Korea Briefing, 1990

Korea Briefing, 1990

edited by
Chong-Sik Lee

Published in cooperation with
The Asia Society

Deborah Field Washburn,
Series Editor

Westview Press
BOULDER • SAN FRANCISCO • OXFORD

Published in 1991 in the United States of America by Westview Press, Inc., 5500 Central Avenue, Boulder, Colorado 80301, and in the United Kingdom by Westview Press, 36 Lonsdale Road, Summertown, Oxford OX2 7EW

Library of Congress ISSN: 1053-4806
ISBN 0-8133-8009-X
ISBN 0-8133-8010-3 (pbk.)

Printed and bound in the United States of America

The paper used in this publication meets the requirements of the American National Standard for Permanence of Paper for Printed Library Materials Z39.48-1984.

10   9   8   7   6   5   4   3   2   1

Contents

Preface

The Asia Society is pleased to introduce this first volume of *Korea Briefing*, an annual review of domestic and international trends and events in the Republic of Korea. *Korea Briefing* follows upon two other annual reviews published by the Society, *China Briefing*, begun in 1980, and *India Briefing*, which recently published its fourth volume. All three books are copublished by The Asia Society and Westview Press. The Asia Society is a nonprofit, nonpartisan educational organization dedicated to increasing understanding by Americans of Asia and its importance to the United States and the world at large.

Public and scholarly interest in Korea is higher than ever today in the United States. A "take-off" in Korean studies and public education about Korea has occurred. The Asia Society has played an active part in fostering this new interest. In addition to *Korea Briefing* and other publications, the Society sponsors policy studies and public education programs relating to this very important part of Asia.

As this book goes to press, the South and North Korean prime ministers have just met in Seoul at a high level, and a second meeting, in Pyongyang, is imminent. No one can suppose a quick solution to deep-seated issues that still generate high levels of tension. Yet the events of the world continue to surprise us, suggesting that not even strategic arrangements are permanent. In the meantime, South Korea's economy is projected to grow at an annual rate of more than 9 percent in 1990, a respectable advance over the 1989 level. Its experiment in democracy continues to take hold. The nation plays new roles in world affairs. These and other themes are treated in depth in the chapters that follow.

I wish to thank Professor Chong-Sik Lee for commissioning and critiquing the chapters and to express my appreciation to him and the other six authors for their fine job of chapter preparation and revision. The Society is grateful to Susan McEachern and her colleagues at Westview Press for their support of the new series.

Several individuals played significant roles in the preparation of this volume. Asia Society Senior Editor Deborah Field Washburn and Publications Assistant Andrea Sokerka guided the book through the editorial and production processes. Program Associate Scott Snyder provided excellent substantive assistance on particular chapters. Dawn Lawson's editorial skills improved the book enormously. Sung-Jae Oh diligently compiled the chronology and glossary. Special thanks are due to Assistant Director Sherrill M. Davis, who worked closely with the editor and chapter authors from the outset, bringing to this project her own commitment to public education and Korean studies.

K. A. Namkung
Executive Director
Education and Contemporary Affairs Division
The Asia Society
September 1990

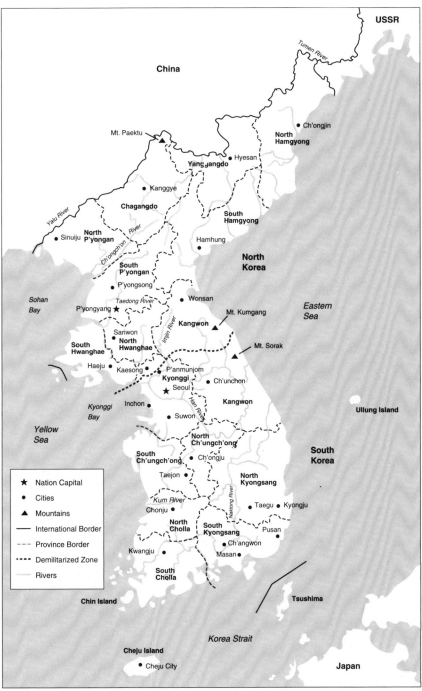

USSR

China

Tumen River

- Ch'ongjin

North
Hamgyong

Mt. Paektu ▲

- Hyesan

Yangjangdo

- Kanggye

Chagangdo

South
Hamgyong

Yalu River

North
P'yongan

- Sinuiju

Ch'ongch'on River

- Hamhung

South
P'yongan

North
Korea

- P'yongsong

Sohan
Bay

Taedong River - Wonsan

P'yongyang ★

Eastern
Sea

Kangwon

Mt. Kumgang ▲

Sariwon

Imjin River

South
Hwanghae

North
Hwanghae

Mt. Sorak ▲

Haeju -

- Kaesong

P'anmunjom

Kyonggi

- Ch'unchon

★ Seoul

Kangwon

Kyonggi
Bay

Inchon -

Ullung Island

- Suwon

Yellow
Sea

North
Ch'ungch'ong

South
Ch'ungch'ong - Ch'ongju

South
Korea

Taejon -

North
Kyongsang

Kum River

Naktong River

- Taegu Kyongju

Chonju -

North
Cholla

South
Kyongsang

- Pusan

Kwangju -

- Ch'angwon

Masan -

South
Cholla

Chin Island

Tsushima

★ Nation Capital
- Cities
▲ Mountains
— International Border
--- Province Border
▪▪▪ Demilitarized Zone
— Rivers

Korea Strait

Cheju Island

- Cheju City

Japan

© Copyright 1990 Asia Society

Introduction

Chong-Sik Lee

We are living in an era of momentous changes. Almost daily we hear about developments that were unthinkable a few years ago. The leaders of the world's seven major industrial nations, for example, met in Houston in July 1990 to discuss the ways and means of providing economic aid to the Soviet Union. The Soviet Union, in turn, agreed not to oppose membership of a united Germany in NATO. East and West Germany have just reunited completely. No one would have predicted these events even a year ago. There is no doubt now that, as far as Europe is concerned, the cold war has ended.

The changes on the Korean peninsula may not have been as dramatic, but many of the events that occurred between 1988 and 1990 can be characterized as historic in the context of Korea's sociopolitical development. The most obvious change was in South Korea's relations with what used to be called the "socialist camp." South Korea established diplomatic relations with all the East European nations (except Albania) in 1989 and early 1990; with the establishment of an official relationship with the Soviet Union in September 1990, South Korea's foreign relations entered a new era.

These developments, of course, affected North Korea, because the Soviet Union and the East European nations had been North Korea's staunch allies since the Democratic People's Republic of Korea (DPRK) was established in 1948. North Korea sharply protested the East European and Soviet rapprochement with South Korea, but in vain. These countries wanted to pursue their own interests rather than follow the dictates of Pyongyang.

Significant changes occurred within South Korea as well. The dismantling of the military-imposed political system in 1987 and the inauguration of Roh Tae Woo as president of the Republic of Korea (ROK) in 1988 marked the beginning of a new era in South Korea's political history. Although one cannot dismiss the military's potential as a political force in South Korea, it no longer plays the dominant role it once did. While not all legal taboos and restrictions have been

1

lifted, the new political system allows the South Korean people the greatest degree of freedom ever in Korean history. Even though there were irregularities in the presidential elections in 1987 and the National Assembly elections the following year, there is no doubt that the voters exercised their rights. The National Assembly is no longer a rubber stamp, and the president can no longer act on his own as his predecessors did for nearly four decades. In short, South Korea underwent its own version of political *perestroika*. These are the subjects of chapters by Sung-Joo Han (politics) and Byung-Joon Ahn (international relations).

South Korea's relations with North Korea have been slow to change, but much has happened recently on this front as well. Chong-Sik Lee's chapter shows that North and South Korea held more meetings and exchanged more communication during 1989 than ever before. Not much happened during the first half of 1990, but in July the two sides agreed to hold a meeting of prime ministers in Seoul in September, to be followed by a similar meeting in Pyongyang in October. Although the Seoul meeting did not go beyond setting an agenda, it represented a major landmark in North-South relations, and there are high hopes that the meeting in Pyongyang will be productive.

The sudden removal of political restrictions greatly affected South Korea's society and economy, as the chapters by Vincent Brandt (society) and Bon-Ho Koo (economy) describe. The students, who had been vociferous even under the draconian regime of Chun Doo Hwan, demanded vast reforms. The workers, whose rights and interests had been restricted, if not suppressed, by the previous regimes, demanded their fair share. Demonstrations and strikes became the norm in South Korea in 1989. Interests and emotions clashed in the open. Manufacturers could not deliver the goods promised, and foreign buyers stayed away. Wages rose, and South Korea lost its competitive edge against other developing economies. Korean economists, however, predict that South Korea's economy will rebound in the latter half of 1990, with a 9.5 percent rise in GNP.

What transpired among workers and students, of course, could not help but inspire writers and artists. Publications of all sorts poured forth. Musicians, choreographers, dancers, dramatists, and other artists became a part of the People's Movement, which reinforced the movements of workers and students. Indeed, there was a renaissance in Korean culture. Freedom became the watchword of this new culture, a welcome change from the rigid and stifling regimen of the previous years. Excitement was in the air. In his chapter, Seung-Kon Kim masterfully records and analyzes the diverse cultural movements in Korea today.

Michael Kalton's chapter, "Korean Modernity: Change and Continuity," attempts to assess all these developments in the context of Korea's history, philosophy, and culture. What role did Korea's Confucian tradition play in its modernization? How did modernization change Korean culture and values? These are some of the questions we asked Professor Kalton to address. Not only those interested in Korea but also students of China, Japan, and other Asian countries will find his analysis insightful and relevant.

The process of change in South Korea between 1988 and 1990 may have appeared to some observers as not only tumultuous but chaotic. Indeed, it was. But the chaos was as inevitable as it was essential for more orderly development in the future. I can say, from the vantage point of September 1990, that in these three years South Korea has virtually completed the period of readjustment and it will now move into a more mature and stable stage.

Note, for example, that the number of strikes declined by 77 percent in the first half of 1990 compared to the same period of the previous year.[1] The workers won a substantial raise in their wages and were promised an improvement in their working conditions. While student demonstrations continue to occur in Seoul and other cities, they no longer generate the kind of passion and enthusiasm they once did among the majority of the student population.

Politics, however, remains volatile as of the time of this writing in spite of President Roh's success in bringing the two opposition parties into a coalition with his party to form a new majority party. (See Sung-Joo Han's chapter for details.) The new Democratic Liberal Party is numerically strong, commanding a two-thirds majority in the National Assembly, but it will take considerable effort on the part of Roh and his colleagues to translate this numerical strength into genuine public support.

---

[1] *Choson Ilbo*, June 22, 1990.

4   *Chong-Sik Lee*

Acknowledgments

I would like to express my deep-felt thanks to each of the authors for their valuable contribution in portraying the dynamic process of change that has been occurring in Korea. The staff at The Asia Society, Sherrill M. Davis, Deborah Field Washburn, and Andrea Sokerka in particular, also deserve more than a perfunctory expression of gratitude. Although the convention does not allow their names to appear on the title page, they should be listed as coeditors of this volume. Special mention should also be made of the contribution made by Scott Snyder, who has added much to the chapters on politics and economy. I am sure the authors will agree that this is truly a joint product of all of us.

Note: Throughout the volume the terms "Korea" and "Korean" refer to South Korea unless North Korea is explicitly included or the time period is before 1948. As to matters of style, we have not followed any strict system of romanization for Korean names but have tried to use the spelling most frequently encountered in English-language publications. Names of persons in the text of chapters are rendered as three separate elements, with the surname first.

1
The Experiment in Democracy

Sung-Joo Han

The Political Background

Korea, along with the Philippines, was at the forefront of a democratic revolution in 1987 that has since swept through Eastern Europe and Central and South America, toppling authoritarian governments and redefining the nature and balance of international relations. As the world began to focus on the 1988 Seoul Olympics scheduled for the following year, businesspeople, workers, and housewives joined student radicals in the streets to demand free elections and an end to the authoritarian government led by former general Chun Doo Hwan. After weeks of escalating tension and confrontation in the streets between fire-bomb-wielding protestors and helmet-clad riot police armed with tear gas, the government yielded to the people's demands.

Roh Tae Woo, a former classmate of General Chun's who had been anointed in April as new leader of the Democratic Justice Party (DJP) and successor to the Korean presidency, declared at the height of the confrontation on June 29, 1987, that the next Korean president would be chosen by the people through free elections under a new democratic constitution, thus launching the Korean experiment with democracy.

This pathbreaking venture truly was an experiment. The only previous democratic revolution, led by student protesters who toppled South Korea's first leader, Syngman Rhee, in April of 1960, had lasted only a year. The popularly elected successors to Rhee, Prime Minister Chang Myon and President Yun Po Sun, were ousted in a military coup d'etat led by General Park Chung Hee. Park imposed a strict authoritarian regime and ruled until he was assassinated by the director of the Korean Central Intelligence Agency, Kim Chae Kyu, in 1979. After months of political turmoil, General Chun took power the fol-

This chapter has benefited from the constructive suggestions of Scott Snyder.

lowing year and bloodily suppressed a popular uprising at the provincial city of Kwangju to consolidate his control. In addition to the precedent of authoritarian rule, Korean culture and tradition are rooted in Confucianism, an ethic that in Korean society emphasizes community hierarchies and social order over individual freedom of expression and self-determination, the central tenets of democratic societies. Roh Tae Woo's June 1987 Declaration was the first step in discovering if democratic reforms were indeed adaptable to Korea, and if so, what kind of democracy Korea would be.

Having ratified a new, democratic constitution in October 1987, the people went back to the polls in December for the first election of a president by direct popular vote in 26 years. Over 90 percent of the people participated in the presidential election, which was won by DJP candidate Roh Tae Woo with a plurality of less than 37 percent of the votes cast. Roh won because the vote for the two long-time opposition leaders, Kim Dae Jung of the Party for Peace and Democracy (PPD) and Kim Young Sam of the Reunification Democratic Party (RDP), was split almost evenly. Kim Jong Pil of the New Democratic-Republican Party (NDRP), a fourth candidate whose party comprised former leaders in the Park Chung Hee government, did much better than expected, capturing 8 percent of the vote. A divided opposition had only itself to blame; the two Kims who led the opposition together received a majority (55 percent) of the votes, yet the DJP, with only a plurality, retained its hold on power.

By early 1988, with Roh Tae Woo's assumption of the presidency, it appeared that South Korean politics might become more subdued after several years of volatile confrontation. A peaceful transition of power had been accomplished, albeit within the same party, through popular democratic elections. With the opposition leadership of the two Kims—Kim Dae Jung and Kim Young Sam—discredited among the electorate for their failure to suppress personal political ambitions and form a united front against Roh, the dominance of the DJP in South Korean politics seemed assured, at least for the foreseeable future.

But the voters handed the DJP an unexpected and serious setback in the April 1988 parliamentary elections. The party failed to secure a majority, winning only 125 seats in the 299-seat National Assembly. Kim Dae Jung's PPD won 71 seats and became the largest opposition party. With Kim Young Sam's RDP and Kim Jong Pil's NDRP securing 59 and 35 seats respectively, the three parties in opposition to the ruling DJP held a substantial majority of the parliamentary seats. The unexpected election results not only resurrected the political lives of Kim Dae Jung and Kim Young Sam but also presented the third Kim, Kim Jong Pil of the NDRP, with disproportionate political influence because he held the balance of power between the government and opposition parties of the other two Kims.

The implications of the composition of the new National Assembly, characterized by *yoso-yadae* (small government party, big opposition), were many and significant. The opposition parties, when they cooperated, could reject presidential nominations, stall budget deliberations, and control the legislative schedule, severely weakening the president's ability to enact his own policy agenda.

Although significant political changes from authoritarian rule to a democratically elected government had occurred during this first year, the successful preparation and hosting of the Olympics became the first priority for politicians and their supporters from both the opposition and the ruling parties. Even so, Koreans experienced drastic sociopolitical changes that were fast in pace and broad in scope. The consciousness and expectations of the people were undergoing a major transformation. Newspapers were freed from government guidelines on what to cover, thousands of political dissidents were released, and long-suppressed labor unions began to organize in order to make demands for improved working conditions against their employers. In an iconoclastic atmosphere of democratization, many of the old values, practices, and institutions were attacked and discredited. Old scores had to be settled; new demands had to be met. The first year was mainly a period of transformation; consolidation of democratic reforms had to wait until the second year.

After the conclusion of the Olympics, the opposition parties went to work by invoking the legislature's investigative powers. They made it the first order of business to investigate and expose the wrongdoings and scandals of the previous regime, the Fifth Republic of General Chun. From October through December of 1988, the National Assembly held hearings in which the Chun government was accused of wrongdoings including, most notably, the violent suppression of the 1980 Kwangju uprising.

Amid revelations of many serious irregularities by the Chun government, including the financial scandals of his close relatives and the existence under his regime of "democratic reeducation camps" for political prisoners, the nation became preoccupied with the "Chun issue"—that is, what to do with the former president. This put President Roh, a close friend of Chun and his primary political beneficiary, in a difficult situation. In addition, President Roh himself was politically vulnerable to rumors that he had been directly involved in the decision to use force in the Kwangju massacre, which had consolidated Chun's control in 1980. President Roh could neither fully protect Chun nor allow him to be prosecuted. In November, a deal was struck between the Chun and Roh camps of the ruling DJP under which the former apologized in a nationally televised address and left Seoul for a self-imposed exile to Paektamsa, a temple in mountainous northeastern South Korea near the demilitarized zone.

Although the opposition in the National Assembly was able to investigate past wrongdoings of the Chun government, divided control of the executive and legislative branches of government meant that little if anything could be done toward legislative reform. Many repressive laws from the Chun era that were incompatible with the newly instituted democratic constitution remained on the books, and other reforms, including the development of local democratically elected governmental administration for the provinces and large cities of the country, were sidetracked.

Despite steady progress toward democracy, South Korean politics revealed several weaknesses that affected future political development. Perhaps the most serious was political fragmentation that denied a stable majority, either in the parliament or as a support base for the president. The society was divided by regions, political orientations, and personalities. The people had spoken in democratic elections, but political power within the parties themselves remained under the control of leaders who continued to invoke authoritarian loyalties and hierarchical structures of dependency among party members.

In dealing with the serious issues of politics, economy, and society, President Roh characteristically let problematic situations deteriorate until it became clear that some drastic action had to be taken. In defense of such a strategy, one could argue that the political cost for the president of heading off potential problems rather than simply reacting patiently was too high. During the first year of his presidency, such a style worked for Roh and for the nation. As the second year of democracy dawned in 1989, however, the people expected their president to demonstrate greater purposefulness and provide clearer direction to the nation. It became apparent that, if the newly won democracy was to survive and thrive, greater efforts toward democratic institution-building had to be made.

The Politics of Reappraisal

One outstanding political issue that had bedeviled President Roh ever since the Seoul Olympics was his campaign promise to ask for a midterm voter evaluation of his administration about a year after assuming office. Although the pledge was not specific, most people understood that Roh would ask for a vote of confidence by referendum. A controversy ensued concerning whether and how the reappraisal should be conducted. Contrary to his promise, President Roh eventually announced in a nationwide television address on March 20, 1989, that he would postpone the reappraisal plan. (Three months later, Roh revealed that he had canceled the assessment altogether.) Indeed, by successfully persuading the people that the postponement was inevitable and maneuvering the opposition parties into supporting the decision, Roh made the retreat look like a political triumph.

In dealing with the reappraisal issue, Roh successfully played on the fears and ambitions of the "three Kims," the opposition politicians who had run against him in the December 1987 presidential election and who were eagerly awaiting a chance to run again. Among those three leaders, each of whom Roh met with separately during the few weeks leading to his postponement decision, Kim Young Sam, the leader of the RDP, was the most insistent that Roh deliver on the promise of a confidence vote by national referendum. Kim Young Sam believed that he himself had the best chance of improving his party's political position and perhaps winning a new presidential election in case of Roh's defeat in a referendum.

By contrast, neither PPD leader Kim Dae Jung nor Kim Jong Pil of the NDRP, the smallest opposition party, regarded such a referendum as in his own political interest. In their view, a decisive victory for Roh would only strengthen the incumbent's hand, drastically reducing the leverage and influence that they already enjoyed in the *yoso-yadae* configuration in the parliament. On the other hand, in their view, a defeat for Roh could have brought about another presidential election for which they were not ready. Worse yet, it could have resulted in a sociopolitical breakdown followed by forcible bids for power by either the extreme left or the extreme right.

Perhaps the most critical factor that enabled Roh to renounce his promise of a confidence vote was a meeting of minds and interests between himself and his erstwhile political foe Kim Dae Jung. Neither one wanted a referendum, but both were interested in winning over Kim Young Sam's middle-of-the-road following and expanding their respective support bases. Kim Young Sam inadvertently helped foster cooperation between Roh and Kim Dae Jung by jumping the gun in early 1989 and demanding a national referendum on the Roh government's tenure in office. As escalating labor disputes, student unrest, and social violence created a sense of crisis in the society, the public began to feel uneasy about a national referendum. Thus, Roh's sudden turnabout undercut Kim Young Sam and seriously eroded his base of support.

Roh's surprise move worked to the extent that it did only because Korean society itself was experiencing volatility. Widespread labor disputes, student unrest, and leftist agitation throughout the country created a popular sense of crisis. Although different in magnitude and substance, the reappraisal episode was similar in nature and sequence to the events that had led to Roh's June 1987 Declaration and set the democratization process into motion. The backdrop of crisis that underlay the reappraisal debate, the secrecy with which the postponement decision was made, the brinksmanship displayed by Roh, who had suggested until the last minute that the referendum would be held as promised—all these were indications that Roh and his advisers had chosen a modus operandi similar to that of June 1987, a style that included "shock treatment" followed by heroic action or conciliation by the president.

The Roh decision on the reappraisal issue and the way it was made had serious repercussions on the fledgling party system. President Roh's own DJP was affected. Before the announcement, many in the DJP had advocated an early confidence referendum and pushed for what they called a "frontal breakthrough" to overcome the latest political deadlock resulting from the DJP's minority status in the National Assembly. Roh's decision not to conduct the interim test completely ignored their views and angered others in the party who resented the fact that the government now had to be more defensive and accommodating to the opposition in the accounting for the so-called Fifth Republic irregularities that had occurred under former president Chun.

At the same time, the episode provided a precedent for collaboration between Roh Tae Woo and Kim Dae Jung and contributed to division among the opposition, shattering a cooperative system that had existed for almost a year among the three opposition parties. Most important, it prompted Kim Young Sam to seek closer cooperation with Kim Jong Pil. Political forces openly hinted at their desire to regroup as the parties and political leaders sought the political alignments that were in their respective interests.

The Politics of Settling Old Scores

If the interim referendum had been held, one criterion of evaluation of the Roh Tae Woo government would have been how thoroughly and successfully it dealt with the negative legacies of the Chun years. As a member of the previous government, President Roh was politically vulnerable if he did not make efforts to punish prior wrongdoings. To Roh's credit, Chun's two brothers were arrested and received prison sentences on charges of extortion and embezzlement. Also, one of Chun's closest aides, Chang Se Dong, former chief of the Presidential Security Service and later director of the Agency for National Security Planning, was put on trial and received a ten-month jail-term for abusing power during the Chun period. Nonetheless, many criticized the Roh government for making insufficient efforts to settle the issue of the "irregularities" that occurred during Chun's Fifth Republic.

After many months of debate, opposition demands on the Fifth Republic issue boiled down to the following two items: that former presidents Chun Doo Hwan and Choi Kyu Hah (the president during the interim between Park Chung Hee's assassination and Chun's takeover of power in 1980) testify in the National Assembly about Fifth Republic government scandals as well as the Kwangju incident; and that Chung Ho Yong, a member of the National Assembly and a military colleague of Chun and Roh at the time of the Kwangju incident, resign from all public positions, taking responsibility for the violent suppression of the Kwangju uprising in 1980. Considering the magnitude and complexity of the Fifth Republic irregularities, the opposition parties' demands in effect represented a major concession on their part, reflecting their desire to bury the corruption of the previous government in the past.

However, even with the scaled-down demands of the opposition the Roh government could not resolve the issue. One reason was the lack of consensus, indeed the existence of a serious division, within the DJP itself. In particular, Chung Ho Yong and his supporters resisted taking the role of "fall guy" in the political game between Roh and the opposition leaders. Furthermore, Roh was not entirely comfortable with the idea of Chun's testifying in the National Assembly. Inasmuch as Roh was himself a close colleague of Chun when the latter took over power in 1980 and a member of the government inner circle during the Fifth Republic, he had reason to be concerned about the possibility that Chun's testimony, particularly if it was to be given over live telecast, could damage his own image and standing. Much groundwork needed to be done before the opposition demands could be met.

Having set the end of 1989 as the deadline for resolving the issue, Roh and his three political opponents—Kim Dae Jung, Kim Young Sam, and Kim Jong Pil—eventually agreed at the eleventh hour (on December 16th) on a framework for resolving the Fifth Republic issues. An 11-point joint statement by the four leaders contained two key items of agreement: that former president Chun would appear before the National Assembly to answer questions submitted in advance concerning allegations of corruption and abuse of power during his term in office, and that national assemblyman Chung Ho Yong would be forced to give up his legislative seat.

Once again Roh managed to salvage the situation by delaying and making others desperate for solutions. Chung was forced to resign by the force of events that had made him seem to be the only obstacle to the restoration of political stability. Former president Chun agreed to testify, but on the last day of the year so that there would be no drawn-out sessions. In his appearance before the legislature and on nationwide telecast, Chun denied allegations of wrongdoing, and his testimony was interrupted by protesting legislators. However, the ritual of Chun's appearance before the National Assembly made it official that divisive issues from the previous administration were settled and that parties and politicians could concentrate on the real business of politics: maneuvering for advantageous positions in future elections, including the next presidential election scheduled for 1992, and vying for political power.

The Politics of Party Realignment

Once the Fifth Republic issues were settled, the inefficiencies of *yoso-yadae*, in which bipartisan cooperation between the ruling and opposition parties was crucial to effect almost any legislative action, became more apparent. Following many months of speculation that some form of party realignment would occur, President Roh Tae Woo of the DJP and opposition leaders Kim Young Sam of the RDP and Kim Jong Pil of the NDRP announced on January 22, 1990, the merger of their political parties and the inauguration of a new political party, the Democratic Liberal Party (DLP). With more than two-thirds of the seats, the new DLP could easily control the National Assembly, and thus the political power and role of the PPD were dramatically lessened. Even for Koreans, who are used to political dramatics, the announcement of the merger of the three parties that had defined themselves as "conservative"—the DJP, RDP, and NDRP—came as a major surprise. Few had expected that long-time opposition leader Kim Young Sam would join hands with Roh Tae Woo and his government party. The initial reaction of the stunned public to the end of the cumbersome four-party system was generally favorable; however, many people expressed displeasure that a significant political realignment had taken place without popular consultation and approval. The realignment also raised the possibility of new divisions and unpredictability in the political environment in the months to come.

The three leaders claimed that they had agreed on the merger "to realize the historic tasks of democratic development and national unity." But clearly, it was primarily the product of careful political calculations and skillful maneuvering. President Roh Tae Woo enticed the two Kims to join him by mortgaging the succession right of his not-as-yet-apparent heir in the DJP, in the process securing a large majority in the National Assembly and augmenting his reputation as a great conciliator and master politician. The DJP was divided among various factions and leaders who were competing for political domination, succession, and power. But since no single person or group had the upper hand, no one could claim that Roh had given up his or their right to succeed him as president. Roh wanted to improve the effectiveness of his administration during his term in office and provide for a smooth transition in its aftermath. Initially, there had been speculation that the Roh camp might form an alliance with Kim Dae Jung's PPD to counter a potential Kim Young Sam–Kim Jong Pil merger or that the DJP might join an alliance between Kim Young Sam and Kim Jong Pil if such an alliance were to materialize. But Roh opted to take a leading role in the merger, thus becoming a full-fledged partner in a coalition in which he could be considered first among three leading partners by virtue of his position as the president.

Kim Jong Pil, by deferring to Kim Young Sam the honor of being second-in-command of the new DLP, achieved his long-sought goal of joining hands with the government party and increased the chances of his own succession to power. It took almost two years after the April 1988 National Assembly elections for Kim Jong Pil and Roh Tae Woo to form an alliance. But it was an inevitable alliance. Kim Jong Pil's party had always had more in common with the DJP than with the longstanding opposition of Kim Young Sam and Kim Dae Jung. Moreover, Kim and Roh are out of the same mold; they share a military background, an orientation toward conservatism, and experience in government positions. Kim Jong Pil needs support from traditional ruling factions if he is to become a serious contender for power in the future. In the absence of a viable successor to Roh, former DJP factions may turn to Kim Jong Pil to keep themselves in power.

For Kim Young Sam, the merger represented the gamble of a lifetime. By offering to cooperate with the heirs of the Park Chung Hee and Chun Doo Hwan governments, he gave up once and for all his claims to be a leader who opposed in principle cooperation with rulers who had been associated with oppression and military regimes. In return, Kim Young Sam was promised a leading position in the new "government party," a share of the cabinet posts, and a likely turn as chief executive. But the political cost to him and his party supporters could be high. He was criticized for delivering the party and its parliamentary seats to the new ruling coalition without proper consultation with other members of his party in the National Assembly, much less with its rank-and-file members.

Kim Young Sam risked losing the trust of his previous supporters. But his political fortunes prior to the merger had appeared to be on the wane. His party candidates had lost badly to the DJP in the earlier by-elections for vacated Assembly seats, crucial political indicators of party strength. In particular, in the hotly contested by-election for the Yongdungpo, Seoul, district seat held in August 1989, the DJP's Rah Woong Bae, a former minister of the economic planning board, finished first with 38 percent of the vote while the PPD and RDP candidates received 29 percent and 18 percent of the vote respectively. The result had been particularly disappointing to Kim Young Sam, whose party had done much better in Seoul in previous elections. Furthermore, as the parties were gearing up for the elections at the provincial, county, and city levels that were expected to be held in 1990, Kim Young Sam's RDP was running into stiff competition from both the ruling DJP and Kim Dae Jung's PPD. Kim Young Sam thus had a strong incentive to join the ruling party with Kim Jong Pil and Roh Tae Woo, forming a grand conservative alliance.

Kim Young Sam's abdication of his opposition role opened the way for the creation of a new opposition party led by Lee Ki Taek, a former RDP member who had distinguished himself as a sharp prosecutor and tough-minded politician in the National Assembly's investigations of Kwangju and other Chun government wrongdoings. Lee's small Democratic Party (DP) was composed of maverick politicians who were unwilling to join the government and objected to the occasionally heavy-handed style and regional associations of Kim Dae Jung and the PPD.

Kim Dae Jung, for his part, expressed indignation at what he claimed was a political coup d'état that ignored the will of the people. He launched a public campaign to denounce the merger. Before the merger and creation of the DLP, Kim Dae Jung had been making full use of his position as the leader of the largest opposition party. He had cooperated with either the government party or the other two opposition parties, depending upon the circumstances and his own political interests. In March 1989 Kim Dae Jung had encouraged and supported Roh Tae Woo's decision to call off a referendum vote on the president's performance, buying the goodwill of President Roh and earning the image of a moderate and responsible leader. On many other issues, including appointments, budget deliberations, and the Fifth Republic issues, the PPD stood at the forefront of the opposition.

But the primary division between the DJP and PPD had come as a result of the arrest and indictment of Rep. Suh Kyong Won, a PPD member who had been charged in the summer of 1989 with illegal entry into North Korea and meetings with its leaders, including Kim Il

Sung. In connection with this incident, Kim Dae Jung himself was indicted by the government on charges of concealing Suh's trip and accepting money that Suh had allegedly brought from North Korea. Although Kim Dae Jung and his party cried "political persecution," the episode provided added justification and impetus to a grand conservative coalition.

However, the bitter long-time regional rivalry that had existed between Kim Dae Jung, from the province of Cholla, and Kim Young Sam, from the province of Kyongsang, was most likely the primary reason behind Kim Young Sam's choice to collaborate with Roh and Kim Jong Pil rather than remain in the opposition. In any event, Kim Dae Jung emerged as the primary opposition leader. But his continued presence as head of the regionally based PPD appeared to limit his attractiveness to potential supporters from other regions or constituencies. There were continuing suggestions that Kim Dae Jung step aside in the interest of uniting the moderate opposition and pressures on Kim Dae Jung and Lee Ki Taek of the newly created Democratic Party to attempt an opposition merger of their own.

Apart from how this change in the political environment may have affected the fortunes of the old-guard politicians, its more immediate effect was to galvanize the radical dissenters, who had been running out of issues that could attract other constituencies. The merger, which they denounced as a conspiracy of the reactionary right, gave them a timely and welcome rallying cause. The new government party, armed with an overwhelming majority in the National Assembly, seemed ready to deal sternly with dissidents who engaged in confrontational street politics. This possibility placed Kim Young Sam and former RDP members in the uncomfortable position of defending any government clampdown on dissidents. In addition, unilateral action and displays of political power by the powerful ruling party have the potential to escalate political polarization and crisis. This occurred in the summer of 1990 when controversial bills were railroaded through the National Assembly during an opposition boycott and every opposition National Assembly member symbolically resigned his position in protest.

The dilemma that Kim Young Sam's group may face underscores the difficulty that the new DLP could have in staying together for any length of time. The new South Korean coalition party has been compared to the Japanese Liberal Democratic Party, which was formed in 1955 by the merger of two conservative parties. Undoubtedly the stability and longevity of Japanese LDP rule were attributes that Roh, Kim Young Sam, and Kim Jong Pil sought to emulate in the formation of the Korean DLP.

But more differences than similarities stand out. The Japanese Liberal Democratic Party was born out of two parties that had once lived under the same roof. The new partners of the Korean coalition have different roots and have always stood at opposing ends of the political spectrum. What worked 35 years ago in Japan, a basically conservative society with strong feudal traditions that emphasize personal loyalties, may be unlikely to accomplish the same goals in today's Korea with its high social mobility, ideological complexity, and raised political consciousness. It is difficult to expect that a stable and pluralistic factional system can sustain a conservative coalition based on political bosses, patrons, and clients. In Korean politics, even within the new conservative coalition, the cleavages are too deep, ambitions too high, and personal loyalties too changeable for this marriage of convenience to last.

For all its problems, the merger of the three parties into one ruling party has its redeeming value. A stable parliamentary majority can enable the administration to carry out its duties with greater consistency, coherence, and confidence. The merger may also give the members of the old Reunification Democratic Party, most of whom had been in opposition for their entire political lives, experience in the business of governing, perhaps making them more realistic and responsible politicians.

Most important, however, the merger may have removed the walls that had insulated the old-guard politicians in their roles as the undisputed bosses of their respective parties. With the protective walls gone, the roof of the old guards has become vulnerable. New leaders are now more likely to move to the forefront of the respective parties and political groupings. Indeed, there have even been discussions in the ongoing Korean democratic experiment concerning constitutional revisions that would provide for a parliamentary democracy with a prime minister instead of a president. The instigators of the merger and constitutional revision in favor of parliamentary democracy may indeed be initiating political changes in the democratic experiment that are far more fundamental and extensive than they ever intended or imagined.

The Politics of Dissent

The radical students and dissident groups, who had played a central role in the 1961 democratic revolution against Syngman Rhee and had protested against the authoritarian regimes of Park and Chun, were the primary catalyst for the street confrontations that had led to Roh's June 1987 Declaration. Free elections and democratic reforms, however, were only a part of their progressive/radical agenda, and they continued to be politically active after democratic reforms began to take effect. They opposed the Seoul Olympics on the ground that it would perpetuate the division of the country by excluding the North Koreans, who had opted not to participate when their requests for joint hosting of some Olympic events were denied. After the Olympics, radical students returned to previous themes, opposing "American imperialism," insisting on the arrest and prosecution of former president Chun, and opposing the Roh Tae Woo government. Arguing that the United States was implicated in the Kwangju massacre and was responsible for the continued division of the country, they urged the withdrawal of U.S. troops from Korea.

As democratic reforms began to spread throughout society, however, public tolerance of dissidents began to wane. The dissidents had lost their most potent platforms for protest as a result of political and social reforms. With the adoption of democratic reforms, the differing priorities and agendas of the various activist groups became more evident. Left-leaning activists turned to the issue of reunification with North Korea, and their fanatic advocacy of immediate reunification of the country proved to be their undoing. The secret and illegal trips to Pyongyang by Reverend Moon Ik Hwan, a dissident, in March and Im Su Kyong, a student activist, in June of 1989 failed to generate public sympathy and instead contributed to a government clampdown on the radical movement. Moon, an impassioned advocate of reunification of the two Koreas, accepted an invitation that had been issued by Kim Il Sung to individuals in the South, including President Roh Tae Woo and several dissidents. Im was secretly invited by Pyongyang to participate in the International Youth Festival at the end of June. Radical students had demonstrated intensely against a government ban on their participation in the Pyongyang event.

The trips to North Korea by Moon Ik Hwan and Im Su Kyong were disturbing to many South Koreans, probably not because they broke the controversial National Security Law by traveling north; most Koreans thought the law was anachronistic and should be changed. They were disturbed, however, that the acts of Moon and Im seemed likely to set back the progress of North-South Korean dialogue and had the potential to threaten democracy at home by galvanizing rightist groups. They recognized that the trips by Moon and Im played into Pyongyang's scheme of denigrating the Seoul government and sowing dissension within South Korea. The Roh government was still struggling to strengthen its legitimacy while maintaining a balance between the radical left and the rigid right. At such a critical juncture, Moon and Im had dangerously cut into Roh's room to maneuver.

They had also undercut the dissenters whose cause they had championed. Kim Il Sung still evoked more negative than positive feelings among the vast majority of South Koreans. Faced with little choice but to endorse these escapades, the dissidents were in effect moving farther away from the Korean electorate, reinforcing a vicious circle of militancy and isolation.

The student radical movement received a serious blow as a result of the death in May 1989 of seven riot policemen who were trapped on top of a building at Tongui University in Pusan and burned in a fire set by student demonstrators. Later in the year, radical students in Seoul beat to death another student suspected of acting as an informant for the authorities. Previously, student activists had been viewed by the public as idealistic guardians of society's moral and political conscience, but such actions increasingly revealed a movement that was torn from within by rival factions and increasingly isolated from the larger public and even from the general student population.

Yet another arm of the activist groups was composed primarily of radical workers. One of the most notable and politically significant developments in the labor movement during 1989 was the formation of the All Nation Teachers' Union (Chongyojo), formally inaugurated in May in defiance of a government ban. The government responded by refusing to approve what it called an illegal action. Consistent with long-held Confucian attitudes concerning the social role of the teacher, the government argued that, because teachers as educators were public servants, they could not legally organize a bona fide labor union. The story was very similar to what had happened in the 1960s when teachers tried to organize a national union of their own after the fall of the Syngman Rhee government. The only existing national organization for teachers in both instances was the Association of Korean Educators (Taehan Kyoryon), which had as its main function keeping the teachers at the lower levels under the tight control of high educational officials.

Instead of concentrating on pragmatic and purely educational matters, however, the new union advocated the implementation of its own educational agenda, referred to as "true education" (ch'am kyoyuk). Government and rightist groups suspected that this was a code word for left-leaning Marxist or communist ideological education, and the government dealt sternly with those who joined the organization. Thus, within a 100-day period after the national union's organization, some 1,500 teachers were dismissed, effectively stultifying the movement, at least for the time being. Although the union was effectively restrained, fired teachers continued to agitate. Even those who did not join the union or renounced their affiliation recognized the need to have their own independent union. Thus, the government simply postponed a major confrontation with the rank-and-file teachers by using coercive means in dealing with the reappearance of a new teachers' union movement.

The labor movement among industrial workers, on the other hand, moved closer to pragmatic, institutionalized activity within the framework of legal boundaries. The labor disputes in the months and years following President Roh's June 1987 Declaration had three main characteristics. First, most large-scale disturbances took place in large enterprises that could afford, at least for the time being, to pay higher wages and provide other benefits for workers. Second, the workers appeared to be interested primarily in pay raises, greater benefits, and improved working conditions rather than in involving themselves in broader political activities. Thus, such student groups as the National Council of University Student Representatives (Chondaehyop), which called for making "common struggle and solidarity" with striking workers a key activity, failed to establish a firm or lasting link with the labor movement. Finally, most of the labor disputes in 1988 and 1989 were settled with minimum intervention by the government.

But clearly there were serious difficulties involved in institutionalizing labor activity in Korea. The spate of labor disputes in 1988 and 1989 contributed not only to rapid wage increases of more than 20 percent annually but also to production delays, missed shipments, and lost orders. Partly as a result of the labor disturbances, the South Korean economic growth rate dropped from 12 percent in 1988 to less than 7 percent in 1989.

With democratization, labor disputes spread, for workers were now free to demand their share of the economic benefits of rapid industrial growth. Competing unions within each establishment promised and demanded unrealistic pay raises, changes in working conditions, and participation in management. Unions also routinely demanded payment for lost work time. Particularly hard hit were some of the largest enterprises such as Daewoo Shipbuilding, Hyundai Automobile, and Lucky-Goldstar Electronics, where workers demanded a "fair share" of the profits made by the conglomerates through the years. Labor disputes not only drove up production costs but also made it difficult to maintain quality control and meet production schedules.

Eventually, the disputes produced consequences that reduced the bargaining power of the labor unions. First, the gains of workers made Korean products much less competitive, with the result that exports were seriously affected. Second, jobs were lost as investors, both Korean and foreign, were frightened off by higher costs, labor militancy, and currency appreciation. Hence the job market was changing so that the labor unions were deprived of the kind of bargaining power they had enjoyed during the boom period. Finally, labor militancy and its negative repercussions on the economy provided the government with justification for taking stronger actions against labor activities that it considered to be excessive. In December 1989, in a precedent-setting agreement at Hyundai Automobile, the workers settled their dispute with the employer after accepting a "no work, no pay" principle.

Leaders of the merger among conservative parties in January 1990 had justified their actions on the grounds that the resulting political consensus and stability would counter dissenter agitation, student activism, and labor unrest. In a joint statement, President Roh and his partners in the new party said that over the last two years, the nation had learned "the very costly lesson" that the political paralysis of the previous system had left it incapable of effectively meeting the domestic and international challenges confronting the nation. In fact, however, by the time of the merger in early 1990, ideological political dissent seemed to have already reached its peak and street activists appeared ready to join the institutional arena by launching a new political party to voice their concerns.

Earlier in 1989, a broad range of progressive forces including labor unionists, student leaders, dissidents, and other activists had merged into a single coalition and formed the Coalition for a National Democratic Movement (Chonminnyon). While many in the alliance preferred to remain a movement outside of institutional politics rather than to merge into the party, there was clearly a need for a leftist party that could appeal to unionized workers, the urban and rural poor, and progressive middle-class voters and intellectuals. Such a move by radicals toward participation in institutional politics was suggested by the fielding of a candidate, Koh Yong Koo, who ran as an independent in the Yongdungpo by-election in August of 1989. A new party with a constituency composed of activists, unionized workers, and the urban and rural poor would face two main challenges: the inevitable factional and personal friction within an ideological party lacking a recognized leader, and the difficulty of winning seats in elections. In a political culture in which votes are decided primarily by personal relationships and considerations other than issues and ideology, progressive parties have always done poorly relative to their strength in the streets, factories, and schools. Perhaps the merger of the three conservative parties will strengthen the cause of a progressive party and enhance its chances of becoming an institutionalized political group.

Conclusion

By the autumn of 1990, South Koreans could look back on their three-year democratic experiment with both a sense of accomplishment and concern. On the one hand, they could take pride in the fact that, after many years of authoritarian rule, democracy with its accompanying freedoms had been restored. In 1988 they had successfully staged the Seoul Olympics. Their international horizon had suddenly broadened as South Korea's relationships with the socialist countries expanded. By a stroke of good fortune, South Korea was at the forefront of the wave of peaceful democratic transition and political liberalization that swept through Eastern Europe and South America in 1989.

On the other hand, South Koreans remained concerned about the slow progress of democratic institution-building and the volatile effect, at least in the short run, of newly won democracy on the economy, law and order, and social stability in general. Local governmental autonomy for provinces and cities, which had been promised by the ruling and opposition parties alike, is yet to be implemented. Political parties are unstable and politics remains volatile. Democratic legal reforms have yet to be carried out. Labor-management disputes and other forms of social strife have had serious repercussions on trade and economic growth. Ideological conflicts have intensified. And there is a growing concern about social disorder and lack of discipline as democratic reforms take root.

Having accomplished much and facing new concerns, the Korean people and their leaders continue their democratic experiment, seeking a political balance that combines a respect for the values of Korean tradition with the freedom of democratic expression. The goal is to achieve a uniquely Korean formula that yields healthy politics, wise policy, and effective government.

2
Foreign Relations: An Expanded Diplomatic Agenda

Byung-Joon Ahn

After the 1988 Seoul Olympics, which provided South Korea with a major opportunity to enhance its international status, the South Korean government set out to practice a more comprehensive diplomacy with security, prosperity, and unification as its goals. With the help of timely developments both domestic and international, the country has achieved considerable success in fulfilling these aspirations.

Developments that have enhanced Korea's ability to act abroad include the reforms in socialist countries, the new détente in East-West relations, and democratization in South Korea. At the same time, there have been limiting factors: the initiation by the United States of a review of the military strategy of maintaining troops in South Korea and Asia, the rise of protectionism in the United States and among members of the European Economic Community (EEC) and other industrial countries, the intransigence and isolation of North Korea, the rise of anti-American feeling in South Korea, and an economic slowdown in South Korea.

These developments have provided the setting for President Roh Tae Woo's efforts to shape an active foreign policy designed to maximize his country's national interests. In the area of security, his government has continued to maintain its alliance with the United States and endeavored to gain the political support of other powers. In the economic realm, Seoul has worked to secure its interests in its trade negotiations with the United States, to promote economic cooperation among the Pacific Rim nations, and to diversify its trading partners throughout the world. It has also made intensive efforts to achieve results from its *Nordpolitik*, that is, its policy toward the Soviet Union and other communist countries, while at the same time trying to resume dialogue with North Korea with the goal of reducing tension and working toward eventual reunification.

An analysis of its foreign relations over 1988–89 reveals that South Korea has succeeded in strengthening its security relationship with the United States through annual consultations and military exercises, but it has also become aware that, because of the U.S. strategy review of the role of U.S. troops on the Korean peninsula, a reconsideration and readjustment of the relationship is necessary. In its trade relationship with the United States, although South Korea was not placed on the list of "foreign priority countries" that might face trade sanctions, it still needed to negotiate agreements regarding the trading of specific commodities. Seoul has made progress in expanding its markets in the EEC and especially in socialist countries. It has become far more active in the encouragement of economic cooperation in the Pacific Rim, one evidence of which is the success of its proposal to host a meeting of the area's foreign and trade ministers in 1991. One of South Korea's more dramatic recent successes is the upgrading of its relations with the communist countries from *de facto* to *de jure* cross-recognition. The future challenge for South Korea is to devise a coherent foreign-relations strategy that will coordinate its security, trade, and Northern policies.

Security Relations

Adjustments in the South Korea-U.S. Relationship

South Korea and the United States have agreed on the need for a U.S. military presence on the peninsula as long as there is a threat to peace and stability and as long as the Korean people support it. The United States has reaffirmed its security commitment to South Korea repeatedly, for example at the 20th Security Consultative Meeting in June 1988 and in President Bush's February 1989 address to the Korean National Assembly. However, because of budgetary and trade deficits in the United States and the mood of détente in U.S.–Soviet relations, it is clear that adjustments will have to be made in the South Korea–U.S. security relationship. These adjustments, which will reflect the outcome of Washington's strategy review and negotiations with Seoul, will affect both sides. The United States will allow South Korea equality and independence in strategy formation and command structure, including operational control over the Korean army, and South Korea will grant the United States concessions in troop reduction and share the economic burden of maintaining U.S. troops on the peninsula.

At the 21st Security Consultative Meeting, convened in Washington in July 1989, South Korea agreed to assume a greater share of the maintenance expense for U.S. troops. This vow was reiterated by President Roh during his October 1989 visit to the United States. However, this did not silence the voices in the U.S. Congress demanding increased sharing of the burden. The present level of South Korean support totals US$300 million in funds and US$1.9 billion in goods and services, including rent, manpower, and electricity.

More serious than the requests that South Korea shoulder more of the economic burden, however, are the demands in the U.S. Congress for reduction or complete withdrawal of the U.S. troops in Korea. Senator Carl Levin (D-Mich.) has proposed a gradual reduction of the current level of 43,000 military personnel, and Senator Dale Bumpers (D-Ark.) has proposed a withdrawal of 10,000 personnel by 1992. In November 1989 Congress passed the so-called Nunn-Warner amendment, in the fiscal 1990 Defense Authorization Act, which required the Bush administration to report to the Congress by April 1, 1990, on the role of U.S. troops on the Korean peninsula and whether they can be withdrawn.

American proponents of withdrawal cite various rationales. One is that the détente in U.S.-Soviet relations makes it unlikely that Moscow would use North Korea to foment a war with the United States. Another is that South Korea's economy is now strong enough to support its own defense capabilities. They also claim that many South Koreans oppose the U.S. military presence, and they contend that a withdrawal would bring about better relations between the Koreas as well as between Pyongyang and Washington; Pyongyang has consistently demanded the withdrawal of U.S. troops as a precondition to a peace agreement with Washington that would replace the existing armistice.[1] (North Korea refuses to sign a peace treaty with the government in Seoul, which it does not recognize.)

South Koreans favoring the withdrawal of U.S. troops represent a small minority, however. In fact, when President Roh addressed a joint session of Congress on October 18, 1989, he cited an opinion poll that reported that 94 percent of South Koreans supported the U.S. military presence, adding that on this issue even South Korea's opposition parties were in agreement.[2] The widespread consensus on this issue stems from the predominant South Korean view that U.S. troops are the most effective deterrent against aggression as long as the North poses a threat. In fact, the primary role of the U.S. Second Division, which is stationed between the Demilitarized Zone (DMZ) and the city of Seoul, home to one-fourth of the South Korean popu-

[1] *International Herald Tribune*, June 30, 1989, p. 3.
[2] *Korea Herald*, October 19, 1989.

lation, is to deter invasion by the North Korean People's Army. It is estimated that over 60 percent of the North Korean army has been deployed along the DMZ, which is located about 40 miles from Seoul, leaving South Korea very little time to be warned of an invasion.

Another important function of U.S. troops on the Korean peninsula is to monitor North Korean military activities. This is particularly crucial to South Korea in its position of defender against an aggressor. Finally, the U.S. presence in South Korea symbolizes the latter's commitment to remain an Asian power, a regional role that is considered essential to the preservation of a balance of power in East Asia.

There are other security questions to be considered by Seoul and Washington, among which are changes in the structure of the Combined Forces Command and its deployment and development of defense technology.[3] Issues on which the two countries have already reached agreement include South Korea's *Nordpolitik*, to which Washington has lent its support, and COCOM (Coordinating Committee for Export to Communist Areas) rules on technology transfer, which Seoul pledged to honor in a signed agreement with Washington in April 1989.

Although there is a general consensus in South Korea on the need for a U.S. military presence there, anti-American feeling coexists with the acknowledgment of that need. Some of this feeling dates back to the 1980 Kwangju incident in which many civilian South Koreans were killed by South Korean commando troops. Many of their fellow citizens felt that the United States was responsible for the use of South Korean troops during the uprising. This reaction was mitigated to some extent by the release in 1989 of the U.S. State Department's detailed reply to a query made by the South Korean National Assembly Committee investigating U.S. involvement in the incident. This document absolved the U.S. commander of responsibility. The anti-Americanism stemming from the Kwangju incident was lessened further when, after former president Chun testified before a National Assembly committee on December 31, 1989, Ambassador Donald Gregg visited Kwangju to discuss the reopening of an American cultural center there.

The anti-American feeling remaining in South Korea today is of two types. The first is based on the belief that the United States is responsible for the division of Korea and, consequently, for all of the nation's problems. Advocates of this view are few in number but highly vocal and fervent in their belief. The second type of anti-American

---

[3] *Korea at the Crossroads: Implications for American Policy* (New York: Council on Foreign Relations and The Asia Society, 1987), pp. 35–50.

sentiment, which is manifested in the resurgence of Korean national-ism and populism, consists of criticism of the visibility of the U.S. presence in South Korea and resentment of U.S. pressures to open Korea's beef and cigarette markets. Because this type of anti-Americanism stems from self-confidence, it may become more preva-lent as South Korean politics and society become more stable.

In an effort to reduce anti-American feeling, Seoul and Washington have agreed to lessen the visibility of the U.S. presence and to deal with some of the Korean War's more undesirable legacies. To these ends, negotiations have begun on the removal of the 8th Army Head-quarters at Yongsan base in the heart of Seoul, and an agreement has already been reached regarding the returning of the base's 18-hole golf course to the city in 1990. In addition, the Status of Forces Agree-ment, which governs the trials of American GIs by South Korean courts, is in the process of revision. Another issue requiring consider-ation in this context is the existence of the Armed Forces Korea Net-work, a U.S. Army television station that is received throughout South Korea. In U.S. diplomatic dealings with Pyongyang, which have been taking place at the counselor level in Beijing since the end of 1988, Washington has been consistently supportive of Seoul, in-forming Seoul of such contacts before they take place and refusing to talk with the northern capital or accept proposals for tripartite talks without Seoul's approval. Washington advocates a direct dialogue be-tween the two Koreas without preconditions. It has endorsed Seoul's new unification formula, announced by President Roh in September 1989, which calls for the building of a united Korean community by restoring cultural and economic exchange before attempting an ulti-mate national reintegration.[4] Washington has also represented Seoul's views on relations between the two Koreas in its bilateral negotiations with Beijing and Moscow.

South Korea's Relationship with Japan

South Korea's relations with Japan have improved, largely because Tokyo regards the peace and stability of the Korean peninsula as es-sential to the peace of Northeast Asia, including Japan itself, and has followed the U.S. initiative of promoting security there. Former Prime Minister Takeshita attended the inauguration of President Roh in Feb-ruary 1988 as well as the opening of the Seoul Olympics in September of that year. Roh made a state visit to Tokyo in May 1990; on this oc-

---

[4] *Korea Herald*, September 12, 1989.

casion, Emperor Akihito apologized to Korea by expressing his "deepest regrets" for Japan's colonial period.

An important ongoing issue in Seoul's relations with Tokyo concerns the legal status of Korean residents in Japan. If they have been granted a term of residence of one year or more they are required to register as aliens within 90 days of the beginning of their term of residence and renew this registration every 5 years. Fingerprinting is required both at the time of initial registration and at all subsequent registrations. Koreans in Japan are also discriminated against in employment and education. In spite of these unresolved issues—and a trade imbalance—Seoul and Tokyo have continued to sustain a correct, if not intimate, political relationship based on the security concerns they have shared for many years.

In 1988 South Korea and Japan established 21st Century Committees, groups of distinguished leaders assigned to study and recommend long-term policy to their respective governments. Also important are the private, unofficial networks of communications that exist among scholars, businesspeople, and other prominent individuals in South Korea, the United States, and Japan and that contribute enormously to the development of an understanding of the many crucial security and political issues faced by these three nations. Seeking opportunities to articulate the foreign policy issues that concern them the most, South Korean scholars have been active sponsors of academic conferences with their counterparts in the United States and Japan.

Economic Relations

Trade with the United States

Because the United States is South Korea's largest trade partner, this economic relationship is of the utmost importance to South Korea and forms the basis for its economic relationships with other countries as well. South Korea being its seventh largest trading partner and the second largest purchaser of its grain, the United States is also aware of the importance of the relationship. Over the years 1986–89, the United States received approximately 38 percent of South Korea's exports, and South Korea recorded a trade surplus with the United States each year. This surplus has led the United States to exert pressure on South Korea to open its markets. Largely because of its intense negotiations and lobbying in Washington during May 1989, South Korea was not designated a Priority Foreign Country, that is, one felt to be deliberately erecting barriers to American exports, by the United States Trade Representative (USTR) under Section 301 of the U.S. Omnibus Trade and Competitiveness Act of 1988. This respite proved brief, however, because the country was placed on the "priority watch list" for intellectual property rights violations, also compiled by the USTR. In September 1989, USTR Carla Hills, Secretary of Commerce Robert Mosbacher, and Vice President Dan Quayle visited Seoul to stress the importance of free trade in the context of U.S.-South Korean relations. Earlier that year, Seoul had promised to reduce tariffs on some 200 agricultural products, eliminate restrictions on certain food items, liberalize investment processes, cut prices of imported cigarettes by almost 50 percent, lift its import ban on beef, lower wine imports, and protect the patent rights of about 700 U.S. products. Such promises did not, however, allay U.S. concerns in those areas, and further dissatisfaction was expressed regarding South Korea's proposal to open its communications market in 1992, a process that the United States had hoped would begin in 1990. Lifting the import ban on beef is anticipated to be difficult for Seoul, because all political parties are committed to protecting the interests of farmers, who have become increasingly anti-American in the wake of these recent developments. One manifestation of these sentiments occurred in February 1989, when about 15,000 farmers attempted to march into the National Assembly building in protest against U.S. pressure to open the agricultural market and other issues.

Despite these domestic difficulties, South Korea is aware that U.S. pressure will not ease until the trade deficit is drastically reduced. As a result, it has taken macroeconomic measures as well, including the raising of the value of the won by 10 percent in 1989 and a deliberate expansion of domestic demands to increase imports.

Another notable source of South Korean ill feeling in the context of its trade relationship with the United States is its belief that Americans regard South Korea as "another Japan." South Korea's gross national product (GNP) is about 6 percent of Japan's, which in fact grew 5.7 percent, or roughly the size of the entire South Korean economy, in 1988. In addition, South Korea is liberalizing its market more rapidly than is Japan.

Trade with Japan

South Korea's trading relationship with Japan is undergoing a shift from a triangular pattern of trading involving those two countries and the United States to a multipolar pattern involving other partners, such as Southeast Asian countries, China, and even the Soviet Union. The realignment in the dollar-yen exchange rate is contributing to this shift because some of the Association of Southeast Asian Nations (ASEAN) countries, such as Indonesia, Malaysia, and Thailand, have begun to behave like newly industrialized countries (NICs), while the NICs (South Korea, Hong Kong, Taiwan, and Singapore) are gradually gaining access to Japanese markets. The result is a horizontal division of labor among multiple actors.

In the traditional triangular pattern, South Korea imported industrial plants and intermediate goods from Japan and used them to manufacture goods for export to the United States. South Korea has had chronic trade deficits with Japan, however, largely because of structural differences and Japanese restrictions. The steady appreciation of the yen has helped mitigate this tendency because Japan has increased its imports of South Korean manufactured goods to save labor costs, and its consumers are increasingly finding Korean-made electronics cheaper and usable. In 1988, for example, South Korea exported US$12 billion worth of products to Japan and imported $US16 billion worth, for a deficit of US$4 billion. There is a possibility that South Korea–Japan trade will be balanced in the near future, and thus the traditional triangular pattern will yield to the multipolar one described above.

Southeast Asia and Pacific Cooperation

In the years since 1980, when South Korea was an initiating member of the Pacific Economic Cooperation Conference, it has sought to secure its economic interests in the Pacific Rim and break out of diplomatic isolation. To these ends, in November 1988 President Roh made state visits to Malaysia, Indonesia, Brunei, and Australia, in the course of which he discussed issues concerning bilateral relations with the respective countries as well as the promotion of economic cooperation in the Pacific.

In July 1989 the ASEAN annual ministerial meeting invited South Korea to be "a sectoral dialogue partner" for trade, investment, and tourism. By not including South Korea as a participant in the 11-country postministerial meeting, ASEAN was offering it less-than-full membership, but South Korea accepted and participated in a working meeting with a delegate from ASEAN to establish a joint commission on trade. In November of that year, Australian Prime Minister Bob Hawke convened a ministerial meeting on Asia-Pacific Economic Cooperation (APEC) in Canberra to discuss trade. In spite of the reluctance of some ASEAN members, South Korea was invited, along with ministers from the usual 11 countries of ASEAN's postministerial meeting. Foreign Minister Choi Ho Joong and Trade Minister Han

Seung Soo attended, expressing their hope for open and outward-looking trade in the region. They also received an affirmative response to their invitation to hold the third meeting of APEC in South Korea in 1991.

In addition to diplomatic initiatives, South Korea has also contributed foreign aid and investment to countries in the region. In 1987 it launched the Economic Development Cooperation Fund to help third-world countries; Indonesia and Nigeria were the first recipients of this aid. In 1989 the investments of South Korean companies in Southeast Asian countries totaled US$276 million.

South Korea perceives itself as playing several roles in Southeast Asia and the Pacific. As a middle-income state, it can function as an intermediary, bridging the gap between economic giants like Japan and the United States, on the one hand, and Southeast Asian countries fearing domination, on the other. In addition, as a prototype of the NICs it is able to represent other Asian NICs while reconciling the differences between the ASEAN countries and Organization for Economic Cooperation and Development (OECD) members in the Pacific. It can also serve as a conduit to nations farther north, such as China and the Soviet Union, which are eager to join the network of Pacific interdependence.

Trade with Members of the EEC

In 1989 Seoul had its sixth high-level consultation with the EEC. Both sides agreed to establish residential missions; the EEC's opened in Seoul in January 1990. In November 1989 President Roh visited France, the United Kingdom, West Germany, Hungary, and Switzerland. One of the purposes of the trip was to present South Korea's views on a variety of economic issues, including the increasing number of protectionist restrictions that the EEC had been placing on South Korean electronics. In response, French President Mitterand promised to increase the quotas for television sets and other electronics products. Chancellor Kohl indicated Bonn's willingness to support Seoul's quest for economic cooperation with the EEC. Prime Minister Thatcher agreed to increase the volume of bilateral trade with South Korea.

In 1988 a team of South Korean economists participated in a seminar sponsored by OECD. With democracy beginning to take root, South Korea intends to join OECD after its securities market has opened sufficiently. There is widespread speculation that it may succeed in this goal and become the first of the Asian NICs to join this elite club.

Nordpolitik

South Korea's increased economic strength has brought it remarkable diplomatic success in its policies toward China, the Soviet Union, and other communist countries. For the first time since 1948 some of these countries have established diplomatic relations with South Korea, and others have set up trade offices there.

Hoping to enhance security, stimulate a dialogue with North Korea, and develop markets for trade and investments, the Roh administration has made special efforts to improve relations with the communist countries. As Roh has indicated in various statements, including his October 18, 1988, address to the United Nations General Assembly, enhancing security and easing tensions with the North are his country's most pressing short-term goals.

Before the 1988 Olympics, Seoul accommodated the communist countries' preference for separating politics and economics because of their political ties with Pyongyang. Afterwards, however, it began to seek to link economic cooperation to the initiation of political relations. The East European countries were quick to initiate political relations, and the Soviet Union eventually followed suit. So far China has consented only to economic relations.

Relations with Eastern Europe

Hungary was the first of the East European countries to establish diplomatic relations with South Korea, doing so on February 1, 1989. When this announcement was made, South Korea pledged Hungary US$120 million in commercial loans. In an address to the parliament during his November 1989 visit to Hungary, President Roh stressed a new spirit of reconciliation and partnership.

Yugoslavia, Czechoslovakia, and Bulgaria opened trade offices in Seoul after the 1988 Seoul Olympic Games. After the opening of the Berlin Wall on November 9, 1989, Poland established diplomatic relations with South Korea, on which occasion Seoul promised that nation US$400 million of Export-Import Bank loans and US$50 million of Economic Development Funds. Although it did not receive economic aid, Yugoslavia established diplomatic relations with South Korea in December. In January 1990 Czechoslovakia agreed to an exchange of ambassadors in March; Romania and Mongolia followed suit in May.

South Korea's trade with the East European countries gradually gained momentum after the Seoul Olympics. In 1988 it exported US$87 million worth of goods to these countries and imported US$79 million worth; in 1989 the volume reached US$400 million. South Korean conglomerates invested US$46.5 million in Hungary alone that year. As East

European countries adopt pluralism and shift to market economies, South Korean trade and investment there will doubtless increase.

Relations with China

Although South Korea has long wanted to develop substantive economic and political ties with the People's Republic of China, the PRC has tended to adhere rigidly to its policy of maintaining a political alliance with North Korea while developing mostly sports-related and economic ties with the South. In spite of this, South Korea and China have become one another's fourth largest trading partners. As their economic, cultural, sports, and personal relationships intensify, there is speculation that Sino-South Korean relations may eventually become political through the creation of trade offices and the initiation of other forms of direct contact between the two governments.

It is important to note that initially, contact between South Korea and China was prompted by unanticipated crises, such as the 1983 hijacking of a Chinese airliner. On that occasion, representatives of the two governments conducted direct negotiations in Seoul to resolve the issue and signed a memorandum concerning future cooperation in the event of similar incidents. Since that time, the South Korean consul general and the New China News Agency in Hong Kong have been engaging in discreet contact. When a Chinese torpedo boat drifted to a South Korean port in 1985, the two countries were able to negotiate to settle the dispute.

Sports-related exchanges have been taking place between the two countries since the late 1970s. In the 1986 Asian Games held in Seoul, China won first place over South Korea's second by just one gold medal. China's participation in the 1988 Seoul Olympics provided an opportunity for the two countries to intensify their economic and social ties.

The most dramatic improvement in Sino-South Korean relations has been in the economic arena. The volume of trade between the two has grown rapidly and dramatically, from US$19 million in 1979 to US$3.09 billion in 1988. The increased competitiveness of South Korean goods since the appreciation of the yen and the complementarity between China and South Korea have contributed greatly to the expansion of their bilateral trade. South Korea exports manufactured goods such as electronics, steel products, synthetic fibers, and chemical fertilizers, while importing Chinese resources such as silk, cotton yarn, coal, and oil. As Vice Premier Tian Jiyun is said to have told a visiting Japanese delegate, by trading directly with South Korea and

Taiwan it can pit South Korea against Japan and even against Taiwan to draw the maximum benefit.[5]

Unlike trade, however, investment has been slow, for a variety of reasons. At the end of the 1980s, only about 20 joint ventures, involving some US$24 million, were in progress, the best known being Daewoo's Fuzhou Refrigerator Company, which began production in June 1988. The small number of joint ventures is not due to lack of interest on the South Korean side. Several South Korean conglomerates and small companies are interested in investing in China as an alternative source of markets. But they face a multitude of difficulties. The lack of diplomatic relations makes it exceedingly difficult for Seoul to negotiate agreements on legal protection for investment, exemption of dual taxation, repatriation of profit, and dispute resolution. Added to these are China's capricious economic policy and irrational price system, unstable political situation, bureaucratic inertia, corruption, and its shortage of infrastructure and competent manpower. Furthermore, South Korean businesspeople are unable to obtain visas for China in their own country, nor are they permitted to take direct flights there. In August 1989 Korean Air made one symbolic flight to Shanghai to carry an athletic team, but negotiations on opening direct flights have failed to make further progress.

After the June 4 massacre in Tiananmen Square, there was a temporary cooling in Sino-South Korean economic and cultural exchange, as indicated by the China Council for the Promotion of International Trade's (CCPIT) abrupt request that the International Private Economic Council of Korea postpone a mission to Beijing scheduled for September 1989 to negotiate the establishment of trade offices. Recently, however, there have been reports that Beijing has again authorized CCPIT to negotiate the matter with another South Korean organization, the Korea Trade Promotion Association (KOTRA).

Not surprisingly, the new Chinese leadership reacted positively to North Korean President Kim Il Sung's visit there in November 1989, at which time it committed itself to defending socialism in the face of the recent fall of various communist regimes in Eastern Europe. In spite of its pro forma endorsement of Pyongyang, however, Beijing's views on security and unification have in actuality tended to be in agreement with Seoul's, supporting peace and stability on the peninsula and advocating a dialogue between the two protagonists as the best means to that end. Future developments in Sino–South Korean relations will depend on Chinese domestic politics: if the Chinese do

---

[5] *Tonga Ilbo*, March 10, 1988.

resume their reforms, it is likely that they will accept some form of South Korean trade office with consular functions.

Relations with the Soviet Union

With the establishment of a consular relationship with Moscow in December 1989, South Korea's relations with the Soviet Union moved a step beyond its relations with China. The Soviet Union's interests in South Korea are primarily economic: in addition to the advantages to be gained from the complementarity of Siberia's rich resources and South Korea's manufacturing skills, it believes that it has much to learn from South Korea in the financial, trade, technological, and educational realms. South Korea, on the other hand, while interested in economic cooperation, is more affected by thoughts of the Soviet influence on its relationship with North Korea and related security issues.

After Hungary opened a trade office in Seoul in June 1988, Moscow began allowing Soviet trade officials and South Korean business representatives to exchange visits. A dramatic initiative was made by Chung Ju Yung, founder and honorary chairman of the Hyundai Business Group, when he went to Moscow in January 1989 to discuss economic cooperation. He reached an agreement with the chairman of the Soviet Chamber of Commerce, Vladislav Malkevich, regarding the establishment of a Soviet-South Korean cooperation committee and subsequently traveled through Siberia to negotiate the development of joint ventures in the timber, fishery, and shipbuilding industries.

In February 1989 Vladimir Golanov, deputy chairman of the Soviet Chamber of Commerce, visited Seoul to conclude an agreement with the president of KOTRA, Lee Sun Ki, on the establishment of trade offices. The increase in such exchanges of visits by business leaders was temporarily interrupted because of conservative reaction to the unauthorized visit to Pyongyang by Reverend Moon Ik Hwan in March. In April, however, the Soviet Chamber did open an office in Seoul, and KOTRA followed suit in Moscow in July.

In August 1989, Chung Ju Yung led a 31-member economic mission to the Soviet Union. Soviet officials expressed their wish that factories be built in the Soviet Union to produce consumer goods and process fishery products, as well as their desire that hotels be constructed in Khabarovsk and that some of their country's military industries be transformed into civilian ones. After bartering some of their raw materials for manufactured goods, they called on Korean business leaders to develop joint ventures.

The Hyundai Business Group has been at the forefront of South Korean economic cooperation with the Soviets. It has signed an agreement with Eduard F. Grabovskiiy, general director of the Forestry Office of the Maritime Province of Siberia, concerning logging and wood processing in Siberia. The 30-year agreement calls for a 50–50 joint venture with initial funding of US$105 million. One million square meters of timber are to be cut in the Svetlaya area annually, an amount that represents 10 percent of South Korea's annual lumber imports.[6] Work began in April 1990.

With South Korea exporting consumer goods and importing raw materials, its trade with the Soviet Union increased dramatically in the 1980s, from a total of US$48 million in 1983 to US$278 million in 1988 and more than US$600 million in 1989. In 1989 direct banking and shipping became possible.

A host of factors has hindered the further development of joint ventures in Siberia. Among these are the lack of diplomatic relations, the fact that the Soviet Union sends military supplies to North Korea, the inconvertibility of the ruble, and Siberia's harsh weather and remoteness. South Korean businesspeople have also made it clear that without some tangible form of legal protection for their investment they are extremely reluctant to venture their capital in remote places in Siberia.

With these difficulties in mind, and contending that it is difficult to issue visas and carry out legally binding negotiations with trade missions, Seoul has insisted on direct negotiations for the establishment of either consular or full diplomatic relations. In November 1989 a compromise was reached that allowed for the establishment of "consular departments" within the semiofficial trade offices. Staffed by diplomats and functioning as embassies in everything but name, these offices began operation in December 1989. The South Korean Foreign Ministry's assignment of a senior officer, Gong Ro Myong, who was formerly consul general in New York City, to the new consular department in Moscow is one indication of the importance Seoul is attaching to this relationship.

There have been other signs of the improving relations between South Korea and the Soviet Union, notably in the area of direct personal contact. Unlike the Chinese, the Soviets have discreetly allowed contact with South Koreans at both official and unofficial levels: in August 1988 an assistant to President Roh reportedly carried a letter to President Gorbachev, and in December 1988 the latter sent a letter to President Roh through an ethnic Korean academician.[7] Another compelling example of this sort of contact occurred in June 1989,

---

[6] *International Herald Tribune*, December 30–31, 1989–January 1, 1990, p. 13.
[7] *Far Eastern Economic Review*, August 10, 1989, p. 29.

when an overture was made to Kim Young Sam, president of the opposition Reunification Democratic Party, by Evgeni Primakov, who
was then director of the Institute of World Economics and International Relations (IMEMO). During his busy campaign for the Supreme
Soviet elections, Primakov had a private talk with Kim and arranged a
meeting between Kim and Ho Dam, Pyongyang's former foreign minister and now a Politburo member in charge of North-South Korean
relations. An increasing number of Soviet scholars, businesspeople,
journalists, and officials have traveled between the two countries
since 1988. In September 1989 Georgy Arbatov, director of the Soviet
Union's Institute for the Study of Canada and the U.S.A. and Mikhail
Kapitsa, director of its Institute of Oriental Studies and former vice
foreign minister, attended seminars in Seoul. The following month
Vladlen A. Martynov, director of IMEMO, led a 12-member delegation to Seoul to participate in a seminar with Kim Young Sam's party.
On June 5, 1990, President Roh had a summit meeting with President
Gorbachev in San Francisco, and on September 30, 1990, the two
countries established formal diplomatic relations.

In addition, Moscow has decided to allow the approximately 36,000
ethnic Koreans who have been living in Sakhalin since the 1930s to
visit South Korea and has even granted permission to some to return
permanently. This process began in December 1988, when the Soviet
Embassy in Tokyo started helping those Koreans obtain visas through
Japanese intermediaries. In June 1989 a group of South Korean legislators went to Sakhalin to discuss this matter. These discussions were
continued in August, when a team of South Korean Red Cross Society officials traveled to Sakhalin to explore the question of repatria-
tion. By the end of 1989, television stations in Seoul and Sakhalin
were using a rare broadcast technique to enable Korean relatives in
the two locations to converse. These humanitarian exchanges were especially meaningful in light of the fact that Pyongyang has yet to allow its millions of families to correspond, much less to visit, with
South Koreans.

In January 1990, when a volcano erupted near Anchorage, Moscow
permitted Korean Air to fly through Soviet airspace en route to Europe. Direct flights between Seoul and Moscow started in April 1990.
Korean Air plans to schedule a weekly stop in Moscow en route to
Europe and to route eight other flights to Europe through Soviet airspace weekly. Aeroflot is to have two weekly flights to Seoul via Beijing and Shanghai and another to Singapore via Khabarovsk and
Seoul.[8]

---

[8] *Far Eastern Economic Review*, January 18, 1990, p. 12.

Although Moscow's official stand on the Korean peninsula continues to be supportive of Pyongyang, several prominent Soviet scholars and commentators have spoken out for cross-recognition and a direct dialogue between the North and South.

Conclusion

South Korea's new comprehensive and independent diplomacy has achieved considerable success in enhancing security and establishing economic and political interests throughout the world. It is expected that South Korea's foreign relations will continue to grow, in breadth as well as depth. For this to happen, however, South Korea must adjust to changes in its domestic as well as its international environment.

First of all, South Korea's foreign policy must be redefined in the light of changes in international alliances and adversarial relationships. Specifically, South Korea's concern for local deterrence must be harmonized with U.S. concerns about global détente. In this context, there is a urgent need for coordination of Seoul's defense policy with Washington's desire to withdraw some of its troops. Any new formula that is developed must of course be dependent on Pyongyang's attitude toward confidence-building measures, such as exchanges of visits and joint economic ventures, and the attitudes of both sides toward arms control.

Domestically, these tasks call for a new policymaking mechanism. At present, Seoul's highly fragmented approach and personalized style of leadership make it difficult for policymakers to design coherent national strategies. In addition, there is no central organization to carry out long-term planning, research, coordination, and evaluation.

Finally, the period when consensus could be built on anti-communism and unilateral reliance on the United States has passed, and a new consensus on important foreign policy issues must be reached. In this age of instant communication and economic interdependence, international politics is being domesticated and domestic policies internationalized. Effective management of domestic political issues is essential for the efficient conduct of foreign relations. The South Korean government must conduct its foreign relations in a way that will, first and foremost, gain the active support of a majority of its people.

3
North and South Korea:
From Confrontation to Negotiation

Chong-Sik Lee

Nineteen eighty-nine will long be remembered as the year the Berlin Wall was torn down and other tumultuous changes occurred in Eastern Europe. The sight of tens of thousands of East Germans streaming past the artificial barricade that had prevented their free movement for decades has surely been indelibly engraved on the minds of people all over the world. For the Germans, unification is finally a reality.

The Koreans (at least those in South Korea, where the news was aired) wistfully watched the epochal events in Germany and other parts of Eastern Europe, wondering whether such events could be replicated in their native land. But they knew too well that there were few, if any, parallels between Germany and Korea. The situation in the two countries had been different from the time when each was initially divided, after World War II. Although millions of East and West Germans have visited each other over the years, only once, in 1985, have private individuals been permitted to travel across the truce line at the 38th parallel that has divided Korea into two parts since 1945; nor has there been any direct exchange of mail. It has not even been possible for family members separated by the truce line to ascertain whether their relatives in the other part of Korea are still alive. East and West Germany have long been engaged in trade, but there has been no exchange of goods between North and South Korea. East Germans and other Eastern Europeans have been watching Western news on television and listening to Western radio broadcasts virtually unhindered for years, but, except for a few select officials, North Koreans have been completely isolated from external news. Eastern Europe has been dominated by the Soviet Union, where President Gorbachev launched the *perestroika* movement, but the North

Korean government has strongly asserted its independence and brooked no outside interference.

Background

What most distinguishes the division of Korea from that of Germany is the warlike atmosphere that prevails in Korea. Although a truce agreement was signed between North Korea and the United Nations Armed Forces Command in 1953 to end the fighting that had broken out in June 1950, the Korean War has never officially ended.[1] Large armies face each other across the truce line, ready to spring into action at a moment's notice. These front-line units engaged in frequent skirmishes throughout the 1970s. North and South Korea tend to view each other as mortal enemies—with suspicion, hatred, and fear. Although the two governments have engaged in unification talks since 1971, the level of tension remains high. In October 1983, while President Chun Doo Hwan was on a state visit to Rangoon, Burma, bombs detonated by North Korean agents killed a number of South Korean officials, including four cabinet members. Moreover, the improvement of U.S.-Soviet relations has had no appreciable effect on the relationship between the two Koreas. Given that both the division of Korea and that of Germany were brought about by the United States and the Soviet Union in 1945, the contrast between the two divided countries was indeed striking.

This contrast was due largely to the nature of the leadership in North Korea, formally known as the Democratic People's Republic of Korea (DPRK). Even though Kim Il Sung emerged as North Korea's leader in 1945 under the auspices of the Soviet army that occupied North Korea between 1945 and 1948, he became increasingly nationalistic in the mid-1950s and began to diverge from the Soviet point of view after 1960, during the Sino-Soviet disputes, in which North Korea increasingly took China's side.

To Kim Il Sung, the only leader North Korea has known since 1945, unification of the nation and the establishment of communism throughout Korea has been a sacrosanct mission. He began advocat-

---

[1] Since South Korea did not send a delegation to the truce talks at Panmunjom between 1951 and 1953—because the South Korean president opposed the truce—the North Koreans argued that the peace treaty should be signed by North Korea and the United States, without South Korean participation. By presenting this argument North Korea has been implicitly denigrating South Korea as a puppet of the United States that does not deserve to be treated as an equal partner with North Korea. This, of course, is not acceptable to South Korea. A peace treaty that did not involve South Korea would be meaningless, in any event.

ing the "liberation" of South Korea in 1946 and has never deviated from that position. He almost succeeded in that task in 1950, when his army launched the war against South Korea, but U.S. intervention stopped him. Kim has stated that it is the presence of U.S. forces in South Korea that prevents Korean unification, and he has insisted that tensions can be eased only if those forces are withdrawn and armaments on both sides reduced. (At the request of the South Korean government, which fears a North Korean attack like the one in 1950, some 43,000 U.S. troops are stationed in South Korea.)

The South Korean government had matched North Korea's obduracy on the unification issue until 1960, but then the situation changed. Syngman Rhee, the president of the Republic of Korea (ROK) between 1948 and 1960, had insisted on destroying the North Korean communist regime by war or any other means possible, but his successors have taken a pragmatic attitude toward reunification. Their governments have advocated a gradual approach that calls for the addressing of the least complicated problems first, followed by a step-by-step progression to more difficult issues as the two sides establish better communication and a deeper mutual understanding. According to this plan, the humanitarian problem of divided families would be addressed first, followed by nonpolitical issues such as trade. Political and military concerns would come later. The South Koreans have tended to believe that the formula for unification offered by North Korea is merely a scheme to weaken the defenses of South Korea before subjecting it to communist assault.

North-South Relations in the 1970s and 1980s

In spite of the high level of tension on the peninsula, North and South Korea have engaged in intermittent talks since 1971, raising hopes that the two sides may eventually be able to accommodate each other. On July 4, 1972, representatives of the two governments dramatically announced that the two sides had agreed on some basic principles for Korean unification and decided to set up a "North-South Coordinating Committee" to prevent armed clashes, facilitate exchanges, expedite Red Cross talks, and resolve the unification issue. The euphoric reactions to this announcement soon faded, however, when it became apparent that there were unbridgeable gaps between the two sides on specific issues. Agreeing on general principles had proved to be far easier than implementing them in specific areas. The committee's second session, held in March 1973, did not even yield a joint statement.

In 1980 representatives from both sides participated in ten preliminary sessions, the ostensible purpose of which was to arrange a meeting between the premiers of the two regimes. President Park had been assassinated in October 1979, and North Korea evidently wished to test the inclinations of the post-Park regime in Seoul. Ascertaining no real change in the ROK's attitude toward North-South relations, however, North Korea terminated the sessions. These 1980 exchanges were still of great significance, because for the first time ever each side referred to its counterpart by its official designation, that is, DPRK or ROK. Although it can be argued that each side had implicitly recognized the existence of the other by engaging in talks since 1971, explicit recognition had been avoided.

In September 1984, South Korea accepted from North Korea a gift of 7,200 tons of rice, 100,000 tons of cement, 500,000 meters of fabric, and 759 boxes of medical supplies for its flood victims. Both the offer and the acceptance of these gifts were clearly politically motivated, and the unprecedented exchange prompted the two sides to return to their dialogue. Economic talks resumed in November of that year, Red Cross talks concerning the reunion of divided families resumed in May 1985, and the representatives of the North and South Korean parliaments initiated contact in July 1985. That October, representatives of athletic societies from both sides held talks in Lucerne, Switzerland.

The two Koreas took a more dramatic step toward reconciliation in September 1985 by facilitating the reunion of 50 families who had been separated in the aftermath of the Korean War. The televised broadcasts of these tearful reunions inspired the entire nation with a heightened desire for freedom of movement and unification. No similar event has taken place since, however.

Negotiations were terminated the following January, when North Korea alleged that the joint military exercises between the South Korean and U.S. forces (code named "Team Spirit") were aimed at North Korea and thus created an atmosphere that was not conducive to unification talks. (It is interesting to note, however, that the same exercises had not prevented North Korea from engaging in talks with South Korea in 1979, 1980, and 1984.) Tensions escalated further in November 1987, when a midair explosion on a Korean Air Lines flight en route from Baghdad to Seoul killed 115 people. A North Korean agent who had deplaned in Bahrain and been arrested there confessed that she and an accomplice had planted the bomb.

With the Olympic Games scheduled to take place in Seoul in September 1988, there was an impetus for both sides to return to the negotiating table. The South Korean government under Roh Tae Woo was apprehensive about the possibility of North Korean sabotage and strove to convince North Korea to participate in the games. North Korea, for its part, wished to cohost the event. Although intense negotiations were held through the International Olympic Committee, a compromise proved unattainable, and North Korea became one of the few nations in the world that did not send a team to the Olympics that year. In July 1988, additional interparliamentary talks were initiated by North Korea, but these were similarly unproductive.

Acknowledging the Need for Coexistence

North and South Korea had nevertheless taken important steps toward the improvement of their relationship in 1988. In that year Kim Il Sung signaled a major change in his attitude toward North-South relations by announcing his acceptance of the principle of coexistence. And Roh Tae Woo reversed his country's longstanding policy of opposing contacts between its major allies, the United States and Japan, and North Korea and agreed to engage in talks with North Korea about military matters.

The ideological shift manifested in Kim Il Sung's statements about the coexistence of North and South Korea was arguably the most significant change that had occurred on the Korean peninsula with regard to the unification question. For many years Kim had steadfastly maintained that the only legitimate government on the Korean peninsula was the one he headed and that the South Korean government had to be overthrown by any available means. His November 1954 statement on the subject had been unambiguous.

The idea that Korea could be separated into Northern and Southern parts and that the parts should coexist is very dangerous; it is a view obstructing our efforts for unification. Those holding this view would *relegate the responsibility of revolution in South Korea to the South Korean people and relieve the people in North Korea of the responsibility of liberating South Korea. This is nothing more than a justification for the division of the Fatherland and for perpetuation of the division.* [Emphasis added][2]

Kim Il Sung opposed coexistence as contrary to the fundamental purpose of his Korean Workers' Party. In April 1955 he said that "the ultimate aim of our party, which is a new form of Marxist-Leninist party, is not only to bring about the unification of the fatherland but

---

[2] "On Our Party's Policies for the Future Development of Agricultural Management," November 3, 1954, *Kim Il-song sonjip* (Selected Works of Kim Il Sung, Pyongyang, 1960), vol. IV, p. 189.

to establish a socialist society and, then taking a further step, a communist society, *throughout the entire nation.*" [Emphasis added][3]

It was, therefore, nothing short of revolutionary for Kim Il Sung to reverse himself on January 1, 1988, and say that North and South Korea must recognize each other's existence. He elaborated on this idea on September 8 of that year when he said: "In order to realize unification . . . we must follow the principle of coexistence and adopt the method of leaving the two systems as they are and uniting them [under a confederation], neither side swallowing or overwhelming the other."[4] As we shall see, however, the North Korean leader has yet to implement his new idea.

The South Korean government had recognized the need for acceptance of the coexistence principle much earlier than the North Korean government. In June 1973 President Park proposed that North and South Korea be simultaneously admitted to the United Nations. Park added that peace must be maintained in the Korean peninsula, that South and North Korea should not interfere in each other's domestic politics, and that no aggression should take place.

Changes in South Korean Policy

Two moves that Roh Tae Woo made in 1988 signified the intensification of his government's conciliatory attitude toward North Korea. The first was a speech on July 7 in which he declared that his government wanted its relationship with North Korea to shift from an adversarial to a cooperative one. He declared that to this end his government would cooperate with North Korea in its efforts to improve its relationships with the United States and Japan. Roh also stated that he would actively promote exchanges of visits between the people of South and North Korea.[5] All of these initiatives constituted a major reversal of previous South Korean government policy.

The other major change in policy toward North Korea was the decision of the South Korean government to include military talks in its dialogue with the North, a decision that was confirmed on December 24.[6] Previous South Korean governments had insisted that military matters should be considered only after the two sides had built trust through other types of contact, but the Roh government evidently felt

---

[3] "On Strengthening the Class Education of Party Members," April 1, 1955, Ibid., p. 225.

[4] *T'ongil Shinbo* (Unification News, Pyongyang), September 17, 1988.

[5] For the text of this speech, see International Cultural Society of Korea, *South-North Dialogue in Korea*, No. 45 (November 1988), pp. 9–12.

[6] *Tonga Ilbo*, December 28, 1989.

that the stage was now set for a simultaneous engagement in all forms of talks, including those concerning military reduction.

The New Policies Interact

Kim Il Sung's acceptance of the principle of coexistence, however, did not signify the North's recognition of the South Korean government under Roh Tae Woo. To the North Koreans, Roh and his government remained merely a "fascist clique" that represented the interests of a minority of the South Korean people and served the interests of American imperialism. In support of this position Kim Il Sung could cite the fact that Roh had received less than 37 percent of the electoral vote in South Korea in December 1987 (his Democratic Justice Party won an even smaller percentage of votes in the election held the following April), whereas he himself has repeatedly been elected by 100 percent of all eligible voters in North Korea.

The North Korean president, therefore, shunned Roh's repeated calls for a summit talk and, instead, called for a conference of representatives of all of the South Korean people. Specifically, he proposed that a conference of representatives of political and social organizations and other prominent figures from North and South Korea be held in 1988 and a "North-South Political Consultative Conference of Leading Personalities" be held in 1989. To the 1989 conference, Kim Il Sung invited the heads of the four South Korean political parties along with three South Korean "notables," whom he specified as Cardinal Kim Su Hwan, a Catholic leader; Reverend Moon Ik Hwan, a dissident Presbyterian leader; and Paek Ki Wan, a former presidential candidate. All three had been sharply critical of dictatorship in South Korea under Chun Doo Hwan; the latter two had denounced the Roh regime as well. It should be noted that Roh was invited as the head of his political party rather than as president of South Korea.

Kim Il Sung had evidently decided to adopt a two-pronged strategy toward South Korea, that is, to continue the intermittent negotiations through official channels but, at the same time, to make a direct approach to the divergent political groups and personalities in South Korea. The latter approach was appropriate from the North Korean perspective because, now that South Korea had evolved into a pluralistic society of diverse elements advocating a variety of views toward unification, any accord reached between North Korea, which is strictly regimented under its supreme leader, and dissident South Korean political groups or individuals would exert pressure on the South's incumbent regime.

The Roh government, on the other hand, was eager to induce North Korea to the bargaining table at any cost short of compromising the integrity of its own authority. Because the 1988 Olympics had prompted South Korea to establish trade and diplomatic relations with many of North Korea's traditional allies, such as China, the Soviet Union, and the socialist nations in Eastern Europe, South Korea was now able to be more assertive in its dealings with North Korea.

Issues Requiring Attention in 1989

Many factors were at play on the Korean peninsula as the year 1989 opened. It was apparent that political leaders on both sides needed to move to reduce tensions and improve relations. In the South, political pressure on the government to modify its confrontational attitude toward North Korea and make more concerted efforts to negotiate continued to build.

North Korea was facing a different set of pressures. On the one hand, it needed to reduce the cost of maintaining its large army and redirect its resources to the civilian economy, which had lagged behind that of South Korea since the early 1970s. The autarchical and Stalinist pattern of economic development based on central planning and an emphasis on heavy industry had been effective in the early stages of postwar reconstruction because it enabled a rapid mobilization of the resources of the country—in fact, the North Korean economy had developed much faster than that of South Korea between 1953 and 1960—but its potential was limited. In the early 1960s, South Korea began to catch up with, and then outpace, North Korea. South Korea's concentration on export-oriented economic development had enabled it to achieve one of the fastest growth rates the world had seen and to transform itself into one of the four "Asian tigers." By the late 1970s, South Korea was clearly ahead of North Korea in terms of technology, productivity, and growth rate.

The North Korean leader had been calling for increased trade with the West since 1975, but his rigid ideological stance and the weakness of his country's economy had made this goal elusive. His government had also attempted to attract foreign investment in its economy by adopting a law on joint ventures in 1984, but its effect thus far had been negligible. It was clear that more fundamental reforms were needed.

North Korea also needed to adjust its foreign policy so that it would be able to break out of its self-imposed isolation. China, the Soviet Union, and the communist countries in Eastern Europe had traditionally been steadfast allies of North Korea, but by now most of them had abandoned their ideology-centered policies and improved their ties with the West. All but one of the East European countries (that is, Albania) established trade and diplomatic ties with South Korea in spite of North Korean protest. The Soviet Union took a giant step closer to South Korea in June 1990, when President Gorbachev met President Roh in San Francisco. Developments such as these underlined the anachronistic nature of North Korean policy toward South Korea. Kim Il Sung's statements about coexistence with South Korea the previous year had been an attempt to respond to his nation's need for change, but it was difficult for the North Korean leader to make a more radical change in policy toward South Korea without altering some of his country's most basic tenets.

For example, the implementation of the principle of coexistence would in theory require a change in North Korea's traditional revolutionary doctrine. But North Korea's policy toward South Korea during 1988 and 1989 showed signs that the North Korean leadership has been unable to resolve the conflict between these two principles. Its strategy of continuing intermittent negotiations with the South Korean government while encouraging revolutionary movements in South Korea suggested that North Korea was following the principle of coexistence without abandoning the cause of revolution. This strategy was a stopgap measure that did not improve North Korea's economy or its foreign relations. Nor did it improve its relationship with South Korea.

New Contacts in 1989

The year 1989 began with dramatic developments that raised many Koreans' hopes for reunification. In January a reporter for Seoul's *Choson Ilbo* (Korea Daily) startled the South Korean citizenry by filing reports from Pyongyang. Until this time South Korean reporters had not been permitted across the border unless accompanying an official delegation.

Chung Ju Yung Travels to Pyongyang

A more dramatic event was a January visit to North Korea by Chung Ju Yung, head of South Korea's Hyundai Business Group. While he was there, Chung and North Korean officials concluded an agreement calling for the joint development of resort facilities at Mt. Kumgang, a mountain on the central east coast of the peninsula known for its extraordinary beauty. North Korea evidently wished to use South Korean technology, capital, and experience to develop its tourist industry. On January 19 South Korea's Ministry of Industry and Commerce announced that other joint venture projects were under negotiation as well. Many believed that peace and unification were at hand because the North Korean regime, which had consistently denounced South Korea for its capitalist economy, now appeared to be willing to collaborate with the South Korean business conglomerate to develop its own economy.

These peaceful initiatives came to a halt on February 8, however, when North Korea announced that the joint military exercises held by South Korean and U.S. forces must end before any further progress on unification could be made. While it may be that, as in the past, the North Korean government intended to force the South Korean and U.S. governments to take into account its attitude toward these exercises, there may have been other reasons for the North Korean action. For example, some elements in the North Korean leadership might have objected to the rapid improvement in relations with South Korea on the grounds that too sudden a change in North Korea's relationship with South Korean capitalists could cause a credibility gap between the government and the North Korean populace, which had for so long been indoctrinated about the evils of capitalism. Or there may have been concern that too rapid a change in North-South relations could spur traditional DPRK allies, such as China, to establish closer ties with South Korea.

Reverend Moon Visits Pyongyang

If the high hopes of January had begun to diminish in February, they were nearly obliterated in March, when Reverend Moon Ik Hwan, one of three dissident "notables" invited to North Korea by Kim Il Sung in January, visited Pyongyang without the authorization of the South Korean government. Reverend Moon's acceptance of the invitation flouted the South Korean law prohibiting unauthorized citizens from communicating with anyone from North Korea. Upon arrival in Pyongyang, Reverend Moon paid tribute to the DPRK president and expressed his basic agreement with the North Korean formula for unification and with North Korea's position vis-à-vis the South Korean regime. Moon's actions generated a harsh reaction by the South Korean government: in addition to deciding to arrest and prosecute Reverend Moon upon his return (he was eventually sentenced to a ten-year prison term, which earned the South harsh denunciations from the North), the South Korean government was prompted to reassess its policies toward the North.

Kim Young Sam Meets Ho Dam in Moscow

The DPRK's initiatives toward South Korea's opposition groups and political leaders continued in June when Ho Dam, a Politburo member and secretary of North Korea's Korean Workers' Party as well as chairman of its Committee for Peaceful Reunification of the Fatherland, contacted Kim Young Sam, the head of South Korea's Reunification Democratic Party, while the latter was visiting Moscow. Ho invited Kim to Pyongyang to meet with the North Korean president, but Kim declined, citing the unfavorable political climate. By so doing, he was echoing the South Korean administration position that the presidents of the two Koreas should have a summit talk to resolve their differences before other political leaders held meetings.

Im Su Kyong Participates in the Pyongyang Youth Festival

Later in June, sensational headlines were made when Im Su Kyong, a 20-year-old Seoul college student, traveled to Pyongyang to participate in the 13th World Festival of Youth and Students, an international athletic meet of representatives of communist nations and organizations. Im presented herself as the representative of Chondaehyop (the National Council of University Student Representatives), a radical South Korean student group.

The South Korean government and the student group had negotiated for months regarding the invitation the student group had received from festival authorities the previous December. The government preferred that student visits take place in the context of general North-South exchanges rather than on an ad hoc basis. It was also concerned that the Pyongyang festival was a political event that would likely be used against the South Korean regime. When negotiations failed, the student group defied the South Korean government and dispatched Im, who traveled surreptitiously to Pyongyang by way of Europe.

During the six weeks from her June arrival until August 15, when she returned to South Korea via Panmunjom, Im was the center of popular attention. Her arrival at the airport in Pyongyang was greeted by throngs of people who surrounded her car as it made its way along the highway to her hotel. At May Day Stadium, a crowd of 150,000 welcomed her with thunderous applause on the opening day of the festival as she marched alone, the sole "representative" of South Korean college students. These events were covered extensively by the mass media in both Koreas.

While in the North, Im stressed the concept of One Korea and advocated reunification. She charged that "American imperialism" and the Roh government were uninterested in unification and even persecuted those who worked toward it. Predictably, she was arrested upon her return to South Korea and lionized by the North Korean media as a Korean Joan of Arc. The South Korean public, however, generally felt negatively toward her. Although many admired her passion and overall bearing, they feared that her activities aided the cause of North Korean propaganda rather than serving the cause of unification.

Assemblyman Suh Kyong Won Visits Pyongyang

While Im Su Kyong was making news in North Korea in late June, the South Korean government announced that it was investigating Assemblyman Suh Kyong Won for visiting North Korea in August 1988 and meeting with Kim Il Sung and Ho Dam. What startled the public was not only that an incumbent National Assembly member was alleged to have made an unauthorized trip to Pyongyang, but also that he had allegedly received US$50,000 from the North Koreans. These revelations had a direct effect on South Korea's domestic politics because Assemblyman Suh was a member of the Party for Peace and Democracy, the strongest of the opposition parties and the one headed by Kim Dae Jung. Kim Dae Jung, who has been the most vocal critic of the Roh regime, has been investigated for possible involvement in Suh's Pyongyang visit.

Official Talks

Red Cross Talks

Although engaging in an intense propaganda war as a result of the incidents recounted above, the two Koreas nonetheless continued their official talks. The Red Cross talks resumed on September 27, 1989, to discuss the possible reunion of separated families and the exchange of artistic troupes. Many observers hoped that both activities could take place within the year, for the first time since 1985, but at year's end no concrete agreement had been reached. The stumbling block was North Korea's insistence on its artistic troupe's performing two opera programs with revolutionary themes. South Korea rejected the two works on the grounds that both extolled the achievements of Kim Il Sung's revolutionary career. Because the family reunions were linked to the artistic exchange, they were thwarted as well.

Sports Talks

The sports talks that had as their purpose the organization of a united Korean team for the 11th Asian Olympiad, scheduled to be held in Beijing in September 1990, proceeded quite smoothly, demonstrating that the two sides could reach a compromise when they had the will to do so. The first round of talks began on March 10, 1989, uninterrupted by the Team Spirit exercises. By November 22, when the sixth session was held, solutions had been found to such thorny questions as the official designation of the united team in Chinese and English, the content of the team's flag, the means of selecting the athletes and the head of the team, and the location of the secretariat. The talks were resumed in January 1990, but after the two sides collided on details of establishing the joint terms, they were terminated.

Interparliamentary Talks

The eighth meeting of the preparatory talks for interparliamentary sessions that had been scheduled for February 1989 was suspended by North Korea because of the Team Spirit exercises. North Korea's June proposal that the talks resume led to a meeting in late October, but this was merely an exchange of acrimonious charges, as was the ninth meeting, held on November 29. The talks continued until the North Korean side terminated them in July 1990.

High-Level Talks

The "High-Level Political and Military Talks" that the DPRK premier had proposed in November 1988 led to five preliminary meetings in 1989, but progress was slow. It wasn't until the last meeting of the year that the two sides reached a compromise on what the high-level talks should be called and who should participate in them. North Korea had insisted on calling the talks "The North-South High-Level Political and Military Talks," while South Korea proposed to call them "The South-North High-Level Authorities' Talks" or the "South-North Premiers' Talks." Clearly the South did not wish to emphasize the military aspect of the talks, although it had agreed on the inclusion in them of chiefs of staff. In the end the two sides compromised on the title "The North-South (or South-North) High-Level Talks." Subsequent talks in July 1990 led to the scheduling of a prime ministers' conference to be held in two installments, the first in Seoul in September 1990 and the second in Pyongyang in October of the same year.

Conclusion

In 1989 extraordinary progress on unification was made in both North and South Korea. Regardless of one's attitude toward the trips to Pyongyang of Reverend Moon and Im Su Kyong, it is indisputable that these actions raised the Korean public's consciousness of the unification issue. Although official talks did not result in a significant improvement in North-South relations, the two sides inched closer together on some issues. Viewed in the light of past negotiations, the results of the sports talks were indeed remarkable.

One should not, however, gauge the extent of change in North-South relations solely by the results of official talks or by the diametrically opposed reactions of the two regimes to the unauthorized visits to Pyongyang by several prominent South Koreans. One marked difference between 1989 and previous years was that the two sides maintained communication in spite of differences of opinion. Because each of the several meetings between the two Koreas presumably required countless telephone calls and other forms of contact, the North and South Korean authorities must have been in constant communication, which in itself is a development of no small significance.

Indeed, in August 1989 the South Korean mass media reported that high-level emissaries from both sides had met in Singapore in January and that a South Korean presidential assistant, Park Chul Un, had visited North Korea twice in June. The two governments were also said to have begun holding secret monthly talks in July 1988 and to have opened a special hotline. Although the South Korean government denied these reports, the allegations were too detailed to be dismissed as mere rumors. Thus, optimism about the prospect of improvement in the relationship between the two Koreas may indeed be warranted.

One reason that improvements in the relationship have been painfully slow to materialize is that the North Korean leader has had difficulty altering his ideological stance toward South Korea. Tumultuous events in Eastern Europe intensified this difficulty because Kim Il Sung could not totally discount the possibility that some of his people might waver from the party line if they were permitted freer contact with South Korea. The North Korean government, therefore, reacted to the events in Eastern Europe by launching an intensive indoctrination campaign among its people. The *Rodong Shinmun* (Workers' News), the official organ of the Korean Workers' Party, for example, reprinted in its December 6, 1989, issue Kim Il Sung's 1958 speech "On Communist Education," which had expounded the virtues of communism and exhorted the people to continue the revolution. As the following quotation suggests, the revolution Kim Il Sung desired was not confined to his own domain:

> The completion of socialist construction in the northern half will not mean the end of our work. There still remain the tasks of reunifying the country and then *carrying out democratic reforms such as agrarian reform and the nationalization of industries in South Korea.* The fulfillment of the tasks of democratic revolution in the southern half should be followed by the continuing task of building socialism, and after the completion of socialist construction, our country will gradually have to move ahead towards communism. Only when all these tasks are carried out with success will we be able to say that we have fulfilled our duties in the world revolution. [Emphasis added][7]

The 1989 indoctrination campaign may have been intended to intensify the North Korean people's belief in the correctness of their leader's revolutionary course, but the reprinting of the text quoted above also served to reveal the disparities between his ideology as expressed in 1958 and his statements about coexistence in 1988. The North Korean leadership may have been ready in 1988 to pay lip service to the principle of coexistence, but it was not yet ready to implement it. But there is still no doubt that the factors that brought changes to Korea in the late 1980s will continue to affect the North-South relationship. The international environment will certainly continue to encourage openness and exchange. Both Koreas recognize the benefit of reducing tension and armaments and both have already taken important steps toward a genuine dialogue. The pace of change is likely to accelerate in the years to come.

---

[7] "On Communist Education," a speech delivered at a short course for the agitators of city and country party committees, November 20, 1958. Reprinted in *Rodong Shinmun*, December 6, 1989. This translation is from the *Pyongyang Times*, December 16, 1989.

4
The Korean Economy: Structural Adjustment for Future Growth

Bon-Ho Koo

During the years 1986 through 1988, the Korean economy had one of the highest growth rates in the world, averaging well over 12 percent. But in 1989 a downturn occurred that was serious enough to concern government officials and the general public. The 1989 growth rate of only 6.7 percent, compared with 13.0 percent in 1987 and 12.4 percent in 1988, is what caught their attention.

The most obvious sign of this economic downturn was the simultaneous decline in the growth rate of exports and manufacturing production; other indications included a sharp decline in the current account surplus and a sluggishness in the overall economy. The volume of merchandise exports registered a negative growth rate of 5.2 percent, compared with increases of 23.7 percent in 1987 and 14 percent in 1988. By contrast, the volume of merchandise imports increased more in 1989 (14.3 percent) than in 1988 (12.3 percent), despite the sharp decline in economic growth. The current account surplus reached US$5 billion in 1989, just over one-third of 1988's US$14.2 billion.

As a result of both domestic and international developments, the need to restructure Korea's economy became apparent in 1989. Before 1989 the Korean economy had relied primarily on export of manufactured goods to achieve growth, but as a result of labor difficulties in export manufacturing sectors, goods produced for export became less competitive on the world market. Simultaneously, trade liberalization allowed South Koreans to meet the long-repressed demand for imported consumer goods. In addition, the United States had heightened its protectionist pressure on Korea to open restricted markets with the implementation of the "Super 301" provision of the U.S. Omnibus Trade Act of 1988. In order to avoid being designated a Priority Foreign Country (one that would face retaliation for unfair trade practices), South Korea implemented a series of measures to repeal regulations on agricultural imports and foreign direct investment as well as to lift nontariff barriers on manufacturing imports. The slowdown of the U.S. economy was an important factor as well, leading to reduced U.S. demand for Korea's exports. The appreciation of the Korean won against the dollar (in combination with the dollar's appreciation against the Japanese yen) further reduced the competitiveness of Korean exports, and domestic labor disputes also contributed to the significant setback in Korea's economic performance.

Adjusting the Korean economy to these changing domestic and international conditions poses many problems for the immediate future and draws complaints from the Korean business community about the exchange rate and the tight monetary and fiscal policies adopted by the Korean government under pressure from the United States. In 1989 sluggish private investment appeared to be eroding the potential for future growth, reduced international competitiveness slowed down exports, and rapid wage increases drove up domestic prices. These adverse developments threatened Korea's ability to sustain stable economic growth, fueling concern that its economy might be heading for a crisis. During the first half of 1990, however, the Korean economy actually reached 9.9 percent growth on the strength of record domestic construction activity and a decrease in labor disputes.

Korea's recent economic transition is partly attributable to the new, more democratic atmosphere that has resulted from the June 29, 1987, Declaration of Democratization and Liberalization by Roh Tae Woo, then the leading presidential candidate from the government party. The suppressed grievances of past decades have burst into the open, and various segments of Korean society are increasingly demanding a bigger share of the "economic pie." Demands for higher wages have shifted the market for Korean exports, requiring them to add value to compensate for higher prices and compete on the basis of quality as well as price.

This crucial period of change can, however, be used as an opportunity to lay the foundations for a new economic takeoff by accelerating industrial restructuring, internationalizing the domestic economy, and improving social equity. Given Korea's potential for sustaining a predicted annual economic growth of 7 to 8 percent through the mid-1990s, the 5.7 percentage points drop in gross national product (GNP) growth in 1989 should not really be cause for alarm, especially since this is an economy that is apparently experiencing a relatively normal downward trend in its business cycle after three years of economic upsurge.

An Overview of Macroeconomic Performance

By any standard, the Korean economy performed remarkably over the 1986–88 period, when the annual economic growth in real terms each year exceeded 12 percent (see Table 1). This figure was unprecedented even for the Korean economy, which had grown annually at a rate of nearly 10 percent over the previous two decades. The main impetus for this remarkable advance came from the manufacturing sector, which grew more than 18 percent in both 1986 and 1987 and 13 percent in 1988.

Merchandise exports grew 26 percent and 24 percent in 1986 and 1987, respectively, and 14 percent in 1988. Fixed capital formation also grew rapidly during those three years. The growth rate of fixed investment more than doubled between 1985 and 1986, from 4.7 percent to 12.0 percent; it was even higher in 1987 and 1988, at 16.5 and 13.4 percent, respectively. Most of this growth came from investment in machinery and equipment, which grew only 5.3 percent in 1985 but jumped to 29.7 percent in 1986. Consumption increased steadily, at a rate of 8 percent in 1986 and 1987 and nearly 10 percent in 1988, although this rate was

TABLE 1.

Macroeconomic Performance

	1985	1986	1987	1988	1989
Real GNP growth (%)	7.0	12.9	13.0	12.4	6.7
Consumption	6.3	8.4	8.1	9.7	9.5
Fixed Capital Formation	4.7	12.0	16.5	13.4	16.2
(Machinery & Equipment)	5.3	29.7	23.5	14.7	13.2
Merchandise Exports	4.4	25.8	23.7	14.0	−5.2
Merchandise Imports	0.3	19.3	20.1	12.3	14.3
Inflation Rates (%)					
GNP Deflator	4.2	2.8	3.5	5.9	4.7
Wholesale Price Index (WPI)	0.9	−1.5	0.5	2.7	1.5
Consumer Price Index (CPI)	2.5	2.8	3.0	7.1	5.7
Current Balance ($ billion)	−0.9	4.6	9.9	14.2	5.0
Trade Balance	0.0	4.2	7.7	11.4	4.6
(Exports)	26.4	33.9	46.2	59.6	61.4
(Imports)	26.5	29.7	38.6	48.2	56.8

Source: Bank of Korea, *Monthly Bulletin*, various issues.

lower than the growth rate of the GNP. The gross savings ratio jumped from 29 percent in 1985 to 38 percent in 1988.

The gap between savings and investment expanded during 1986–88, as did the current account surplus, which totaled 8.4 percent of the nominal GNP in 1988. The expansion in the current account surplus, which peaked in 1988, caused an inflationary pressure in the economy. Having seen its economy suffer from chronic inflation during the 1970s, the Korean government had made price stability its first priority during the 1980s. The effort was successful: the average annual inflation rate in terms of the consumer price index (CPI) was only 2.8 percent in 1986, a figure that is comparable with that of well-stabilized countries such as Japan and Taiwan. The same year, Korea's wholesale price index (WPI) actually declined by 1.5 percent. But the hard-earned price stability of the first half of the 1980s began to be threatened in 1987 and 1988, when the CPI rose 3 and 7 percent, respectively. Factors contributing to inflation in those years included the rapid wage increase and the excess demand for goods that had resulted from the sustained rapid growth in overall economic activities. The steady price rise in service-related sectors and food, especially vegetables and meat, contributed to rising inflation, reflecting the rapidly rising real income of consumers. Particularly damaging were wage hikes and the expectation of continued inflation, factors that must always be contained before they get out of control.

Fixed capital formation grew 16 percent in 1989, indicating a structural shift in the Korean economy. The investment in construction rose substantially, by 19.8 percent. Real consumption grew at a rate of 9.5 percent. Overall, this general picture of Korea's macroeconomic performance in 1989 indicates that the sharp decline in the growth rate was a result of the negative contribution in foreign trade and that economic growth was sustained by high private consumption and investment, particularly in the nonmanufacturing service sectors.

Compared with the performance of the Korean economy in other years, including 1986–88, the year 1989 saw a number of developments that cannot be sustained in the long run. The growth rate of consumption, especially private consumption, was too rapid, exceeding the GNP growth rate by 3 percentage points. The growth rate of imports, especially consumption goods, at more than twice the growth rate of the GNP was also too rapid, especially since exports declined by more than 5 percent. If investment in services and construction replaces manufacturing investment because of the low expected return on the latter, this development will hurt Korea's growth potential.

Exchange Rates, Wages, and Productivity

The shift in expenditures from export-led growth to domestic demand-led growth was motivated by the substantial deterioration of Korea's competitiveness. With the marked appreciation of the won, the sharp increase in nominal wages, and the slowdown in productivity growth, the competitiveness of Korea's exports has become a critical issue. Table 2 illustrates the dramatic improvement of competitiveness with the outside world in 1986 and its rapid deterioration since 1988.

TABLE 2.

Exchange Rates, Wages, and Productivity in Manufacturing

(Unit: average annual change, %)

	1983–85	1986	1987	1988	1989
Normal Exchange Rate (average)	6.0	1.3	-6.7^1	-11.2	-8.1
Real Effective Exchange Rate^2	4.3	14.6	0.9	-8.9	-12.2
Nominal Wage	10.1	9.2	11.6	19.6	25.1
Consumer Price Index	2.7	2.8	3.0	7.1	5.7
Real Wage^3	7.2	6.2	8.0	11.3	17.9
Labor Productivity^4					
Household Survey	7.9	8.5	2.7	7.3	0.0
Firms Survey	11.0	14.2	12.0	12.6	7.9
Unit Labor Cost ($)^5					
Household Survey	-3.7	-0.6	16.4	25.6	36.2
Firms Survey	-6.4	-5.5	6.7	19.6	26.1
Terms of Trade^6	1.2	8.8	2.5	2.8	7.6

Notes: 1. Negative values indicate the appreciation of the won.
2. Provided by Morgan Guaranty Trust, *World Financial Market*.
3. Nominal wage divided by consumer price index.
4. Value added in manufacturing divided by those employed in manufacturing. The trends of employment differ according to the survey method.
5. Unit labor cost in won currency divided by nominal exchange rate.
6. Export unit price divided by import unit price.
Sources: Morgan Guaranty Trust, *World Financial Market*, various issues. Bank of Korea, *Monthly Bulletin*, various issues.

After the Plaza Accord in September 1985, in which the Group of Five (the United States, Great Britain, France, West Germany, and Italy) agreed to intervene in the exchange markets to push down the value of the U.S. dollar against major foreign currencies, the won began to depreciate against these currencies too. When Korea began to record current account surpluses in 1986, however, the won began to appreciate against the dollar, although at a much lower rate than did the Japanese yen or the Taiwan dollar. Specifically, the won appreciated against the U.S. dollar by 6.7 percent in 1987 and 11.2 percent in 1988, figures that can hardly be compared with the major appreciations of the yen—25.4 percent and 31.2 percent—and the Taiwan dollar—12.3 percent and 31.2 percent—in 1986 and 1987. By 1989 the real effective exchange rate for the Korean won (a measure of the amount of actual goods the won can buy) had appreciated to the level it had occupied prior to the 1985 Plaza Accord. The main reason for this appears to be the yen's depreciation against the dollar in the first half of 1989. In light of these developments, Korea must now undertake to adjust its exchange rates against the U.S. dollar and the yen.

Nominal wages in the manufacturing sector were stable between 1983 and 1986, increasing about 10 percent annually. Because the inflation rate during this period was very low—the annual average rate of increase in the CPI was 2.7 percent—the real wage (a measure of the actual purchasing power of wages earned) rose substantially, by approximately 6 to 7 percent each year. During the same period, labor productivity, which is defined as the value added per employee, grew at a rate that exceeded the rate of increase in nominal wages. This led to an average 3.7 percent annual decline in the unit labor cost in dollar terms. All of these factors—price stability, stable wages, high labor productivity, and declining unit labor costs from 1983 to 1986—contributed to the continuing improvement in Korea's external competitiveness.

This positive economic performance began to deteriorate by the latter half of 1987, when severe labor disputes in major manufacturing plants erupted with the formation of radical labor unions. Labor unions had begun to gather strength in Korea in 1987 with the initiation of political liberalization and democratization. Labor disputes led to an 18.6 percent rate of increase in nominal wages in the 4th quarter of 1987. This pattern recurred in 1988, when the growth rate of nominal wages in the manufacturing sector reached 19.6 percent. Value-added labor productivity in the manufacturing sector showed a 7 percent increase when the number of employed was obtained from the household survey, while the unit labor cost measured in U.S. dollars increased 26 percent. In 1989 this latter figure increased 36 percent and nominal wages increased 25 percent, while productivity growth was stagnant. This increase in the cost to companies to produce a cer-

TABLE 3.

Sources of Growth by Industry (1985 constant prices)

(Unit: annual average, %)

	1980–82	1983–85	1986–88	1989
Gross Domestic Product	3.9	9.4	12.0	6.1
Agriculture, Forestry, and Fishing	0.0	0.5	0.2	−0.1
Mining	0.0	0.0	0.0	0.0
Manufacturing	1.4	3.9	5.6	1.2
Construction	0.3	0.8	0.6	1.2
Electricity, Gas, and Water	0.2	0.5	0.5	0.3
Transportation	0.4	0.7	0.9	0.8
Other Services	1.6	3.0	4.4	2.8

Note: Percentage contribution is computed as component's growth rate multiplied by its share in total output.
Source: Bank of Korea, *National Income Statistics*, 1988, 1989.

tain amount of goods created a lessened competitive advantage for Korean companies and a decline in Korean export-led growth as well as in overall economic performance.

The Industrial Structure, Foreign Trade, and Investment

Changes in the Industrial Structure

The rapid growth of the Korean economy during the 1986–88 period and the continuing shifts in the industrial structure were fueled mainly by the export of manufactured goods. As Table 3 indicates, the contribution of the manufacturing sector expanded rapidly through 1988 but recorded a very low 1 percent growth rate in 1989. The production of general machinery, electrical and electronics products, and fabricated metal products also grew rapidly through 1988. Korea's dynamic comparative economic advantage was developed in these subsectors, which had in the past been dominated by industrialized countries.[1]

---

[1] Bon-Ho Koo and Taeho Bark, "Recent Macroeconomic Performance and Industrial Structural Adjustment in Korea," KDI Working Paper No. 8924, August 1989.

Tables 4 and 5 offer clues to the puzzling question of how Korea's industrial structure shifted to become more like those of the industrial countries, where R&D and skill-intensive products such as electronics and machinery predominate. Recently developed products such as semiconductors, VCRs, passenger cars, personal computers and other office automation equipment, microwave ovens, and magnetic tapes for audio-visual and computer use were the key products that led Korea's export growth over the 1986–88 period. Between 1983 and 1985, when the successful policy for price stabilization took effect, the Korean manufacturing industry had invested heavily in research and development, especially of commercial products and their mass production. As shown in Table 5, R&D investment grew at an average rate of 82.5 percent annually between 1983 and 1985. Investment activities in the manufacturing sector were highly concentrated in the electronics and electric machinery and automobile subsectors: during this period the average annual growth rates of R&D expenditures in the two subsectors were 149.8 percent and 168.7 percent, respectively.

Table 4 indicates that mass production of newly developed goods tended to begin a few years after their commercial development. The high absorption capacity of Korea's manufacturing industries, equipped with large numbers of trained engineers and research personnel, and the high level of R&D investment made it possible for export to take place immediately following mass production, however. The extremely high export growth rates of these products is also shown in Table 4.

The Foreign Trade Pattern

During the years 1985–88, the technology and skill-intensive sectors became the Korean manufacturing industry's leading export sectors. As shown in Table 6, the electronics industry exported US$2.9 billion in 1985, accounting for 9.5 percent of total exports. The export value of that industry's products continued to rise over the next several years, constituting 13.7 percent of total exports in 1988. Interestingly, exports from the textile sector, which is known for its production of relatively labor-intensive goods, more than doubled between 1985 and 1988. This dramatic increase is best understood in the context of that sector's large increase in R&D expenditures, shown in Table 5. This increase was accompanied by a high level of investment in new equipment and machinery intended to increase productivity. Consequently, the textile and apparel sectors were now producing skill-intensive goods instead of merely labor-intensive ones. Korea had become a production location for high-quality, mass-produced textile goods.

TABLE 4.

New Exports and Export Trend

(Units: US $100 million and %)

Products	Year of Product Development	Year of Mass Production and Export	Export Trend			
			1986	1987	1988	1989
Semi-conductors	1983–86	1984–87	12.0 (47.4)[1]	18.5 (53.6)	29.2 (57.8)	23.1 (44.8)
VCRs	1979–82	1982	7.5 (118.1)	12.1 (60.8)	17.7 (46.2)	16.3 (−7.5)
Automobiles	1981–84	1985–86	13.8 (155.8)	28.1 (103.8)	35.9 (28.0)	23.2 (−35.3)
Office Equipment[2]	1980	1984	9.9 (68.6)	16.6 (61.3)	25.7 (60.9)	21.3 (8.1)
Microwave Ovens	1980	1982	4.4 (109.5)	6.4 (43.2)	8.4 (33.3)	5.6 (3.7)
Magnetic Tape	1975–82	1980	4.6 (91.9)	5.2 (12.8)	6.8 (32.5)	5.3 (26.2)
Total			52.0 (90.5)	86.0 (65.4)	123.2 (43.2)	76.6 (7.0)
Other Exports			(20.7) 295.1	(31.1) 386.8	(25.1) 483.8	(4.4) 320.3

Notes: 1. Figures in parentheses are composition ratios.
2. Office equipment includes personal computers.
Source: Bank of Korea.

TABLE 5.

Growth Rate of R&D Investment

(Unit: average annual rate of increase, %)

Industries	1983–85	1986–89
Manufacturing	82.5	24.0
Electric and Electronic Products	149.8	20.6
Transport Equipment	168.7	27.9
General Machineries	−19.2	39.7
Textiles	121.3	6.9

Source: Korea Development Bank.

TABLE 6.

Korea's Exports by Major Commodities

(Units: US$ billion and %)

	1985	1986	1987	1988	1989	
Textiles	6.6	8.2	11.0	13.5	14.4	[7.2]²
	(21.8)¹	(23.7)	(23.3)	(22.2)	(23.1)	
Electric and	2.9	4.2	6.4	8.3	9.1	[9.8]
Electronics	(9.5)	(12.0)	(13.6)	(13.7)	(14.7)	
Iron and	3.3	3.4	4.0	5.4	5.8	[7.2]
Steel	(10.9)	(9.6)	(8.4)	(8.9)	(9.2)	
Footwear	1.5	2.0	2.7	3.4	3.2	[−5.5]
	(5.0)	(5.8)	(5.8)	(5.6)	(5.2)	
Automobiles	0.5	1.4	3.0	3.6	2.3	[−35.3]
	(1.8)	(3.9)	(6.3)	(5.9)	(3.7)	
Marine	0.8	1.2	1.5	1.7	1.5	[−13.2]
Products	(2.6)	(3.4)	(3.2)	(2.8)	(2.4)	
Chemicals	0.6	0.7	1.2	1.3	1.3	[9.6]
	(1.8)	(1.9)	(2.0)	(2.1)	(2.1)	
Ships	5.0	1.8	1.1	1.8	1.8	[1.6]
	(16.6)	(5.2)	(2.4)	(2.9)	(2.9)	
Machinery	1.4	1.9	3.3	5.2	5.6	[8.8]
	(4.5)	(5.5)	(6.9)	(8.5)	(9.0)	
Total	30.3	34.7	47.3	60.7	62.4	[2.8]
	(100.0)	(100.0)	(100.0)	(100.0)	(100.0)	

Notes: 1. Figures in parentheses are composition ratios.
2. Figures in brackets are percentage changes compared with the same period of the previous year.
Source: The Office of Customs Administration.

Where were Korea's rapidly increasing export goods bound? Table 7 illustrates the regional pattern of exports and imports from 1986 through 1989. Most continued to go to Korea's traditional markets: the United States and Japan. In 1986 exports to the United States constituted 40 percent of Korea's total exports. By 1988 that figure had declined to a still significant 35.3 percent; this decrease was welcome

TABLE 7.

Korea's Export and Import Share by Region

(Unit: %)

	1986		1987		1988		1989	
	Export	Import	Export	Import	Export	Import	Export	Import
U.S.A.	40.0	20.7	38.7	21.4	35.3	24.6	33.1	25.9
Japan	15.6	34.4	17.8	33.3	19.8	30.7	21.6	28.4
EEC	15.1	10.1	14.0	11.2	13.4	11.7	11.9	10.6
Asian NICs[1]	5.9	3.3	7.8	3.9	9.7	4.2	10.0	4.2
ASEAN[2]	2.3	5.9	2.2	5.9	2.8	5.5	3.8	5.4
Total[3]	100.0	100.0	100.0	100.0	100.0	100.0	100.0	100.0
	(34.7)	(31.6)	(47.3)	(41.0)	(60.7)	(51.8)	(62.4)	(61.5)

Notes: 1. Asian NICs: Hong Kong, Singapore, Taiwan.
2. ASEAN: Malaysia, Thailand, Indonesia, Philippines.
3. Figures in parentheses are export values (Unit: US$ billion).
Source: Office of Customs Administration.

because Korea's trade surplus had become a source of increasing friction between the two countries.

It appears that a gradual diversification in the pattern of Korea's trade is beginning. For example, Korea's price competitiveness and Japan's need for increased manufactured imports resulted in the increase of Japan's share of Korea's total exports to over 21 percent by 1989, from under 16 percent in 1985. In addition, Korean exports to the other Asian newly industrialized countries (NICs) also increased significantly, from 5.9 percent of total exports in 1986 to 10 percent in 1988. This increase is particularly remarkable because the Asian NICs, producers of similar goods with similar levels of industrialization, had not previously traded much with one another. As their industries have become more developed, however, the need for intra-industry trade has become stronger. It is expected that in the future this new pattern of intra-industry trade will expand to incorporate the less industrialized countries of Southeast Asia as well.

Korea's import pattern also changed dramatically during 1986–88. Imports also grew rapidly, if not as rapidly as exports: they increased from US$31.1 billion in 1985 to US$61.5 billion in 1989. The principal reason for this was the strong government effort to liberalize imports. Another reason was the appreciation of the Korean won, which increased the purchasing power of Koreans in the international marketplace. These two factors also affected the pattern of import usage. For example, imports to be used for domestic final consumption increased faster than those to be used as inputs for manufacturing export products. Imports of consumer durables grew particularly fast, although it is important to realize that their rate of growth was calculated from a relatively low base.

The pattern of imports by region also showed significant changes. Imports from the United States increased from just under 21 percent of total imports in 1986 to nearly 26 percent in 1989. Imports from Japan decreased by 3 percentage points during the same period. As mentioned above, imports from the Asian NICs also increased.

Korea's trade with socialist countries, especially China, increased as well, although the low starting base may once again have exaggerated the rate of increase. China and other socialist countries welcomed trade opportunities with Korea, despite the lack of official diplomatic channels. By 1988 Korea was exporting nearly US$2 billion worth of goods to these countries and importing US$1.6 billion worth; the bulk of this trade was with China.

Foreign Direct Investment

As Table 8 illustrates, the inflow of foreign direct investment (FDI) to Korea was substantial over the years 1986–88, reaching nearly US$900 million in 1988. Historically, however, FDI played a limited role in Korean economic development. Annual FDI inflow tended to be less than 1 percent of total capital formation, rarely exceeding 10 percent of long-term capital inflow. This means that the gap between domestic savings and investment was financed mainly by the inflow of foreign loans rather than by foreign direct investment.

Since 1984 the Korean government has adopted a series of liberalization measures that, together with the country's rapid economic growth, have led to a tremendous increase in FDI inflow. Some service sectors not formerly allowed to receive FDI have been opened up and the rules restricting the establishment of wholly owned subsidiaries liberalized. Performance requirements and investment incentives have been reduced significantly and will soon be abolished.

Korea's Investment Abroad

Korea's foreign investment abroad was insignificant until 1982, when it began to increase modestly. Its growth rate has accelerated since 1986. The stock of Korean FDI abroad was US$174 million in

1981 but grew to US$633 million in 1986 and US$1.12 billion in 1988. Two factors explain the low level of Korean FDI before 1986. The first is that Korea ran a significant current account deficit almost every year until then, which indicates that there was a vigorous demand for domestic investment, one that exceeded domestic savings. As a result, the rate of return on domestic investment was quite high. The second factor is that government policy on outward foreign investment was quite restrictive: all Korean investments abroad required government approval. Korea's FDI thus tended to be concentrated in natural resources development projects to meet domestic needs or in trade-related activities.

These factors have changed in recent years. With a growing balance-of-payments surplus, the Korean government liberalized its FDI policy, eliminating many restrictive clauses. This liberalization is part of the government policy encouraging structural changes in Korean industry, which is burdened with rapidly rising domestic wages and the appreciation of the Korean won against the U.S. dollar. Another reason for the encouragement of FDI outflow was protectionist threats from major importing countries such as the United States and members of the European Economic Community (EEC).

TABLE 8.

Trends of Foreign Direct Investment in Korea[1]

(Unit: US$ million)

	Approved FDI		Arrived FDI	Remaining	
	No. of Projects	Investment Amount		No. of Projects	Investment Amount
1986	203	353.8	477.4	1,143	2,865.7
1987	363	1,060.2	625.5	1,444	2,895.4
1988	342	1,282.7	894.1	1,696	4,991.3
1989	336	1,090.3	812.3	1,816	5,424.6
Total	3,090	7,067.1	4,968.9	1,950	6,045.3

Note: 1. The data here are based on a new series released by the Ministry of Finance in 1987. The old and new series differ significantly, primarily because the latter includes the purchase of existing companies. In addition, the new series corrects mistakes made in compilation of the raw data.

Source: Ministry of Finance.

TABLE 9.

Korea's FDI (Stock) by Sector and Region: 1962–1988

(Units: cases and US$ thousand)

Region	Primary Industry	Manufacturing Industry	Service Industry	Total
S.E. Asia				
Cases	9	67	131	207
Amount	166,376	74,126	46,446	286,948
Middle East				
Cases	1	7	29	34
Amount	135,887	17,437	22,416	175,740
North America				
Cases	13	38	198	249
Amount	101,507	252,938	133,292	487,737
Latin America				
Cases	14	25	15	54
Amount	8,437	11,853	5,692	25,982
Europe				
Cases	1	10	54	65
Amount	40	15,855	25,773	41,668
Africa				
Cases	5	6	11	22
Amount	242	8,344	4,200	12,786
Oceania				
Cases	9	15	13	37
Amount	76,200	6,300	5,801	88,301
Total				
Cases	52	168	448	668
Amount	488,689	386,853	243,620	1,119,162

Source: Bank of Korea.

The sectoral and regional patterns of Korean FDI shown in Table 9 indicate that nearly 50 percent of all approved investment went to Canada and the United States and 25.6 percent went to Southeast Asia. More than 40 percent of the total was invested in natural resources development projects, which are located mainly in Southeast Asia, the Middle East, and North America. Korea's FDI stock in the manufacturing industry totaled about US$400 million in 1988. Approximately 70 percent of these projects are located in North America and 20 percent in Southeast Asia. The relative size of Korea's North American projects is fairly large compared with the average size of investment per project, which is about US$6.7 million. In Southeast Asia it is only US$1.1 million. This is because investment in North America is concentrated in large manufacturing operations: Hyundai's automobile plant in Quebec, Posco's steel plant in California, and Samsung and Gold Star's investments in electronics manufacturing plants in New Jersey and Alabama, respectively. By contrast, Korean manufacturing operations in Southeast Asia tend to be small, labor intensive, and mostly directed toward the export market.

As it has increased its trade ties with countries such as China, Hungary, and the Soviet Union, Korea has begun investing small amounts in these countries as well. The approved value of FDI in such countries since 1985 has amounted to more than US$100 million.

Interpretation of Korean Economic Development in 1989

Some of the salient features of Korean economic development in 1989 can be summarized as follows. The growth of economic activities slowed significantly, largely because of a sharp decline in exports and a marked rise in imports. The current account surplus thus declined from US$14.2 billion in 1988 to US$5 billion in 1989. The wholesale price index increased 2 percent and the consumer price index almost 6 percent.

If one considers these factors in isolation, the macroeconomic performance of Korea in 1989 does not appear to be cause for concern. On the contrary, the Korean economy may be considered as healthy as other strong economies, such as that of Japan. Furthermore, although it represents a sharp decline from the double-digit growth rates of 1986–88, the 1989 increase of 6.7 percent in the real GNP is respectable compared to the lower growth rates of other countries in both the developed and the developing world. The current account surplus, corrected from 8 percent of GNP to 2 percent, is at a desirable level. All of the indicators constitute a good performance during the adjustment period following the record growth of previous years. It is possible to view the replacement of foreign demand as the main source of growth by domestic demand as desirable from the point of view of global structural adjustment. Inflation was somewhat high, but not alarmingly so.

Nevertheless, a pessimistic view prevails among some observers of the Korean economy. This is partly attributable to some of the concerns already discussed, such as the decline in real exports after the growth of the preceding three years. This decline is especially disturbing because it is coupled with the rising demand at home for imports rather than domestic products. The growth rate of the demand for imports, particularly consumer durables, has been too precipitous for an economy experiencing a decline in overall activities.

The growth in manufacturing investment was weak in 1989 compared with that of Korea's main competitors, such as Japan and Taiwan. Major investment activities were concentrated in construction and other nonmanufacturing sectors, not a healthy development for the Korean economy, whose export-led growth requires that it maintain international competitiveness in manufacturing.

These problems are closely related. The more than 5 percent decline in real exports in 1989 is the result of a loss in price competitiveness, which in turn is caused by a combination of the sharp increase in wage rates since 1987 (unit labor cost increased by 36 percent in dollar terms in 1989) and the significant appreciation of the Korean won in 1987 and 1988.

Consideration of the political developments in Korea during these years provides insight into the origins of these problems. As mentioned earlier, Roh's June 1987 Declaration initiated a period of rapid change in Korea's political and governmental processes. Democratization meant that the government no longer had a monopoly on deciding national priorities. Popular support was now required for any governmental decision-making, and the government had to respond to the long pent-up demands of various sectors of Korean society. Organized labor's demands for higher wages and improved working conditions affected the economy most seriously. Although the contributions of entrepreneurs and the government cannot be ignored, the backbone of Korea's dramatic industrial development over the last three decades was the excellent performance of Korean workers. Their high rate of productivity was comparable to that of workers in industrial countries, while their low wages were on a par with those of workers in developing countries.

After the Declaration, strong labor unions, especially those based in large plants such as those in the automobile and electronics industry, engaged in serious worker-management conflicts. They demanded a sharp increase in wages, threatening to stop work or to cause stoppages and other disturbances in the nation's major factories. They justified their demands for large wage increases by citing the inflation rate in living essentials, which is much higher than the inflation rate measured by the CPI, and applying it to the purchasing package of a typical worker family. Their newly gained power, coupled with political backing, enabled labor unions to negotiate large nominal wage gains for 1987–89. Because they directly pushed up the cost of production and indirectly pushed up the inflation rate, cutting into real wage gains, these wage negotiations were crucial in eroding the international competitiveness of Korean exports. Despite the substantial growth of nominal and real wage rates, the competitiveness of Korean industry was further eroded by the failure of labor productivity to increase in 1989. As the authoritarian anti-labor political process was weakened through various reforms, worker discipline appears to have slackened. This phenomenon can be linked to the troubling trend toward more unequal distribution of income.

Historically, Korea has had a fairly equitable income distribution compared to other developing countries. This was a result of the export-led growth strategy based on labor-intensive products of the 1960s and early 1970s, which generated numerous employment opportunities for workers. There are some indications that income distribution has become more unequal in recent years, however, mainly because of the lack of an efficient tax system to deal with the huge capital gains obtained by a small percentage of the population through land and stock speculation during the boom period of 1986–88. In addition, the conspicuous consumption pattern of the newly rich is being copied by those who have not experienced a comparable rise in income. The results of this are a reduced propensity to save along with an increased demand for higher wages by labor groups, who argue that greater capital gains for the high-income groups are unfair.

Challenges and Prospects: Structural Adjustment for Future Growth

The complex set of problems discussed above makes short-run economic adjustment in Korea difficult. The serious labor-management conflicts, unequal income distribution, and instability brought on by political change all require long-term solutions; hence the pessimism about the Korean economy's performance in the immediate future. Based on the country's experience over the last quarter-century, however, few dispute that its economy has great potential to resume healthy growth in the long run. With neither abundant natural resources nor large amounts of capital and technology, Korea has always relied on human resources. The importance attached to developing human potential can be seen in the growth of government investment in education; however, government expenditures account for only about one-third of the total expenditures on education, the remainder being borne by the private sector. In addition, public vocational training institutes, in-house training programs by private enterprises, and overseas training have contributed to the development of skilled manpower in Korea.

The labor-management conflicts Korea has experienced over the past two years are an inevitable part of the process of transition from an authoritarian to a more democratic and liberal society. The problem of inequitable income distribution is not insurmountable either, because the Korean populace as a whole is sensitive to it.

Current Policy Reforms

Changes in both the international and the domestic environment require that Korean industry make structural adjustments in order to maintain healthy economic growth and advance into the ranks of the industrialized economies by the late 1990s.[2] Implementing the policies described below will make it possible to achieve these adjustments. First, to strengthen Korea's potential for continued economic growth, the government intends to continue to promote human resource development, particularly of R&D personnel, and to retrain workers as required for industrial restructuring. Second, it will support greater investment in R&D and in the expertise necessary to absorb foreign technology. The government also plans to strengthen private-sector initiatives by increasing market competition through the lowering of entry barriers and increased support of small- and medium-sized industries.

To resolve conflicts between labor and management, their relationship must be transformed into a cooperative one that will achieve the common goal of economic growth. The equitable distribution of profits is a prerequisite for this, and to this end the government plans to overhaul the tax codes, increasing capital gains taxes and discouraging speculation on land and other real assets.[3]

---

[2] To meet domestic and international economic challenges, President Roh established the Presidential Commission on Economic Restructuring for which the Korea Development Institute acted as Secretariat. The commission's report, *Realigning Korea's National Priorities for Economic Advance*, was published by the Korea Development Institute in 1988.

[3] Ezra F. Vogel and David L. Lindauer, "Toward a Social Compact for South Korean Labor," Development Discussion Paper No. 317, Harvard Institute for International Development, Harvard University, November 1989.

Finally, Korea must strive for further internationalization of its economy. The government plans to continue the major policy measures it has already implemented to liberalize foreign trade and investment regimes. As for import restrictions and tariffs, Korea's market is already open to an extent comparable to those of some members of the Organization for Economic Cooperation and Development. In the future, Korea will need to contribute more to the international organizations that support economic growth in developing countries as well as to the individual developing countries themselves.

In conclusion, the performance of the Korean economy in 1989 revealed some serious short-term problems, some of which were closely related to domestic political developments, but the economy rebounded strongly in the first half of 1990 on the strength of significant growth in domestic construction industry. The problems of 1989 will presumably be resolved as Korea's political and economic evolution continues its course and the government learns to manage new problems such as labor-management conflicts. It is projected that in the long run the Korean economy will resume the healthy growth that has been its hallmark, based, as always, on its most important resource: its potential for human development.

5
South Korean Society

Vincent S. R. Brandt

The transformation of South Korean society during the past three decades has astonished the world. Under strict authoritarian direction the Korean people have demonstrated an extraordinary productive dynamism. They have adapted effectively to modern industrial organization and acquired complex technological skills. With a relatively non-ideological, trial-and-error, "can-do" approach to problem solving, the South Koreans have been very effective since about 1964 in achieving their tangible, material goals.

Other popular aspirations have proved more elusive, however, and much of the tension and instability that characterize the current scene reflects widespread discontent with what is regarded as a badly skewed development process. Between 1961 and 1987 South Korean leaders (mainly former generals and bureaucrats) emphasized economic, military, and diplomatic progress, while political democracy, human rights, social and economic justice, and protection of the environment were generally suppressed, ignored, or played down. Since June 1987, however, when most of the demands of the political opposition were accepted in principle, South Korea has become a more open society, with functioning democratic institutions, a relaxation of strict governmental controls, and a considerable degree of freedom of speech and of the mass media. Still more recently, beginning in early 1989, the government has again cracked down on both labor and student protesters, deploying large numbers of riot police and making numerous arrests. In 1990 discontent and protest continued among radical students, in the labor movement, and in opposition political circles.

Underlying these changes has been a transformation in class structure, values, attitudes, occupations, and patterns of behavior. Over a period of only 25 to 30 years, South Korea has made a remarkable shift from a predominantly rural and agricultural past to an overwhelmingly industrial and urban present.

also from Trad ideas to modern ideas:

75

Perceptions, Images, and Reality

Most broad generalizations about South Koreans and their society do not hold up well. Despite a high degree of homogeneity in language, customs, and cultural tradition, South Korea today is an extremely complex place. Although the influence of the Confucian past is still strong in many ways, new values, new ways of thinking, and new patterns of behavior are increasingly dominant. The country is swarming with people, the population is almost 100 percent literate, and the mass media are developed to a point of near saturation. In this social pressure cooker, diversity is as conspicuous as uniformity.

One generalization that does apply reasonably well, however, is that Koreans are goal- and achievement-oriented, continually dissatisfied with what exists today and constantly looking forward to an idealized future. The non-Korean might interpret this as a kind of optimism—the belief that long-term social trends are positive and that children will have a better life than that of their parents. But there is a widespread tendency among Koreans to denigrate the present, with people quickly taking for granted what has already been achieved and longing for more. In the South Korean case perennial discontent has also been a source of productive dynamism, helping to produce the motivation and hard-driving human energy that has resulted in an economic "miracle."

There is today an almost obsessive concern on the part of many articulate Koreans, particularly students and intellectuals, with all that they perceive to be wrong with contemporary life and institutions. And in South Korea, where there is a long and illustrious tradition of government by scholar-officials, intellectuals are extremely influential. It is not only the intensity of such criticism that is striking, but also the fact that it is focused largely on abstract ethical issues. The way authority is structured and wealth distributed, the way institutions function, and above all how persons in high places behave are important not only because they determine whether there will be prosperity, happiness, and national strength; something larger is at stake. The idea of society as the most important expression of a fundamental moral order is more than a dusty aspect of ancient Confucian doctrine. It is of constant, immediate importance—an integral part of popular culture.

In talking to journalists, professors, or the man in the street, or by reading Korean newspapers, a visitor to Korea is likely to obtain the impression that things have reached a disastrous state. According to most current wisdom, crime is rampant, family values are being rapidly eroded in a flood of egoism, businesspeople are predatory and their greed is undiluted by any sense of social responsibility, politicians seek only personal power and wealth without concern for the common good, and bureaucrats are haughty and corrupt. In some accounts militant students are violent and irrational and labor is on the rampage, making excessive demands. Or, alternatively, a repressive regime is brutally stifling the heroic expression of student idealism, and capitalist entrepreneurs in the service of American imperialism oppress long-suffering, exploited laborers. The litany of social evils goes on: the fabric of society is being torn apart because of indecisive leadership; or, continued militaristic and authoritarian rule prevents the attainment of democratic and other reforms. And then the culminating and most comprehensive indictment: the nation, immersed in an orgy of materialistic vulgarity (largely of American origin), is pursuing false goals that are directly at odds with traditional spiritual values.

Then, after listening to all this, the visitor looks around and observes enormous crowds of cheerful, apparently prosperous people. There is plenty of buoyant good feeling along with the turmoil and protest. One sees a population that is energetically enjoying the considerable material rewards of its hard work but that also has one of the highest rates of personal saving in the world. One notes the enormous investment by parents in their children's education and the constant, competitive drive for upward mobility. It appears that South Korea is reaching out eagerly and forcefully in every direction, exploring new diplomatic, technological, commercial, political, and cultural opportunities wherever they exist and making the most of its extraordinary human resources in the process.

Why do things look so good from the outside and so terrible from the inside? Why has the good feeling and pride in national accomplishment that was generated in connection with the 1988 Olympic Games dissipated so rapidly? The answer presumably is that non-Koreans are usually contrasting the present situation with that of 10 or 20 years ago or comparing social indicators in South Korea with those of other developing countries. Koreans, however, seem compelled to contrast the messy, imperfect, inadequate present with an ideal vision of how things ought to be. Not only are expectations high, but there is great impatience if their fulfillment is postponed. Perhaps most of all there is the anxiety and instability that accompanies political ambivalence. Koreans are thoroughly fed up with authoritarian, bureaucratic rule, but making democratic institutions work effectively is proving to be an awesome task.

The degree of dissatisfaction varies a great deal, of course, among the different sectors of Korean society. There is a small ruling establishment, a commercial/industrial elite, and a not-so-small upper middle class, all of whom are reasonably content with the present state of affairs. But certain other sectors or classes are vociferously unhappy, in particular organized labor and militant students.

Koreans may be critical of the current social scene, but they are also well aware of their successes. A cocky, even pugnacious nationalism has replaced the former attitudes of dependency and humility vis-à-vis the advanced industrial world. National pride and self-confidence coexist with agonizingly critical self-appraisal.

The main problem seems to be that rapid change over the past 25 years or so has been uneven, with disproportionate emphasis on economic growth, national security (the military), and the maintenance of political stability. In the 1960s and early 1970s higher living standards and protection from another North Korean invasion were national preoccupations, and, in fact, a considerable degree of consensus developed under former president Park Chung Hee (1961–79) in support of what might be called policies of national survival and economic growth.

By the 1980s and continuing into 1990, however, most Koreans appeared to feel strongly that a decisive correction of the distorted patterns of the past was long overdue and that it was time for major reforms with regard to more pressing ethical issues: democratization and the guarantee of human rights, social and economic justice for all, reunification with the North, and absolute national autonomy. Koreans seem to want balanced, harmonious, rapid, and simultaneous progress toward all these goals, and tremendous popular impatience and anger have been directed at the authorities because of governmental resistance to reform. Although substantial progress has been made by President Roh Tae Woo's new government toward correcting the worst abuses, no one appears to be satisfied. In particular, the belief that wealth and status are unfairly distributed in Korean society has convinced many intellectuals, workers, and students that further fundamental change is necessary. To complicate the situation still further, there is the inchoate but nevertheless deeply held feeling that in spite of all the change the nation must retain its essential identity, somehow holding fast to precious cultural traditions in the face of overwhelming materialistic challenges from outside.

But some of the successes of the past interfere with the desire to move in new directions. For example, the strong centralized militaristic leadership that made an essential contribution to rapid economic growth has inhibited democratic processes. Also, the military and diplomatic dependence on the United States that helped guarantee security against the threat of aggression by North Korea is seen as a humil-

⎛─iating loss of national independence. And, to take a more sociological example, traditional family values and the ubiquitous hierarchical ordering of personal status have been at odds with growing individualism and egalitarian ideals.

The process of rapid development and modernization can be messy, chaotic, and sometimes contradictory. Imbalance, lack of integration, uncertainty, and tension between different value systems are as much a part of it as are rising living standards, astonishing export growth rates, and fair elections.

At the broadest level of analysis two strongly contrasting perspectives on Korean society are possible. The first is that it is a going concern. Tensions, frustrations, and discontents can be regarded simply as growing pains, an inevitable part of social change. As problems arise, solutions are being found. South Korea is in the process of building a new national consensus that comprises democratic pluralism and social justice as well as economic growth and national strength. A lot of the pessimistic commentary by Koreans, however, suggests another, less sanguine perspective: that there is so much divisiveness within Korean society that a more or less integrated national consensus will be unattainable and it will be very difficult to achieve any sort of constructive accommodation between labor and management, between geographic regions, between those who have power and wealth and those who do not, or between those who advocate gradual reform and those who insist on revolutionary change.

My own conclusion is that things are in reasonably good shape. Of course, the apocalyptic view of Korean intellectuals and other critics is part of the scene and must be taken into account. After all, they have a more profound knowledge of the inner workings of Korean society than an outsider can ever hope to acquire. But it is important to bear in mind that they are fulfilling a role, that of society's stern moral conscience, and that some of the sound and fury is merely a matter of style.

Perhaps an analogy can be made between contemporary society and the scene at a Korean provincial bus station. The atmosphere is one of perpetual crisis bordering on disordered frenzy. Buses back up and load and blow their horns in an impossibly constricted space. The drivers are stern autocrats, constantly asserting their status and authority. Men, women, and children carry their baggage back and forth, shouting, quarreling, and laughing. They run to and fro, deeply involved in personal greetings and goodbyes, just barely managing to catch a bus at the last moment. Some try to ride for nothing, and occasional pickpockets rob their fellow passengers. And yet the buses leave on time, carry full loads, and arrive at their destinations. The system is neither tranquil nor elegant, but it works.

Population, Class, and Mobility

As a result of energetic and well-funded family planning programs and the effects of rapid urbanization and industrialization, the population growth rate declined from about 3 percent in 1960 to about 1.2 percent in 1987. The rate of decline now seems to have stalled, however, largely due to a marked national preference for sons over daughters. With a total population of more than 42 million in an area about the size of West Virginia, South Korea is one of the most crowded countries in the world: only Bangladesh and the Netherlands have more people per square kilometer, and both of those countries are far less mountainous than South Korea. By the year 2000, when the South Korean population will exceed 50 million, pressures on living, working, and recreational space will be so great that much stricter and more comprehensive regulation of land use seems inevitable. Similarly, environmental problems are severe and worsening, so that centralized bureaucratic regulation in the areas of conservation and pollution control will have to be intensified. Such imperatives are certain to act as constraints on some aspects of individual and entrepreneurial freedom as well as on the development of local administrative autonomy.

Massive rural-urban migration, together with a dramatic shift in the occupational structure, has accompanied rapid growth. The rural population peaked in 1967 at about 16 million (54 percent of the total population). In 1988 there were fewer than half that many people living in rural villages and small towns, and they made up only 18 percent of the total population.

Most of the old Korean class structure was swept away as a result of the turmoil following liberation from Japanese colonial rule in 1945 (the Japanese formally annexed Korea in 1910), the thoroughgoing land reform of 1949–50, and the enormous leveling effects of the Korean War (1950–53). Nevertheless descendants of such former elite groups as absentee landowners and successful entrepreneurs during the Japanese colonial period, as well as members of the military, bureaucratic, and business elites under President Syngman Rhee (1948–60), have tenaciously maintained a foothold in the middle and upper middle class. They have accomplished this largely through the education of their children and wise investments; their numbers are small, however, relative to the total population.

South Korean population structure has in recent years been characterized by a pronounced "youth bulge," as a result of declining mortality rates and the extended baby boom that followed the Korean War. In 1985, according to census figures, 23 percent of the population was in the 15-to-25-year age group, an extraordinarily high ratio in comparative terms. A number of social scientists have pointed out that there is usually a correlation between such a "youth bulge" and political and social instability, often marked by both organized protest movements and riots. In the Korean case the demographic phenomenon peaked in 1985. The number of young people as a proportion of the total population is now declining fairly precipitously and will continue to do so in the foreseeable future.

Between 1967 and 1988 the number of blue-collar workers more than quadrupled, while there was a similar or perhaps even greater increase in the number of persons employed in urban service jobs. This relatively youthful labor force (about two-thirds of all workers are 30 years old or younger) has until recently been largely of rural origin. Although generally future-oriented, with aspirations toward upward mobility, such young people have generally had a traditional upbringing in small, cohesive, but poor farm communities. For the most part they came to the city imbued with strong family values, respect for their status superiors, an intense work ethic, and generally conservative political views. With newly available industrial jobs as the only alternative to subsistence agriculture, young workers (both male and female) submitted willingly to a repressively paternalistic factory system that required long hours at low wages.

In spite of the large increase in the number of industrial workers (they constitute about one-quarter of all employed persons), 25 years of rapid economic growth have transformed South Korea into a predominantly middle-class nation. Class is a difficult concept to define precisely, particularly where social structure is changing rapidly, as in Korea. On the basis of income and occupation, however, and if we include the skilled blue-collar elite, well-to-do farmers, petty merchants, and entrepreneurs, along with clerical, professional, technical, managerial, and other white-collar occupations, more than half the population can be characterized as belonging to the middle class. With relative prosperity there has occurred a marked proliferation of middle-class lifestyles and expectations. As for self-categorization, recent polls indicate that some 65 to 70 percent of urban Koreans see themselves as belonging to the middle class.

The existence of a preponderant middle-class mentality, along with the private property to go with it, means that most people have a substantial stake in the existing system. Accordingly, they are likely to be strongly opposed to instability or challenges to law and order. This, in fact, appears to have been the case in South Korea until June 1987, when large numbers of younger office workers joined radical dissident students in the streets of downtown Seoul to protest President Chun Doo Hwan's abusive rule (1980–87). It was a dramatic indication of how restive the nation had become. Resentment, anger, and contempt had been building for many years, but it had been assumed that only student activists would take part in violent demonstrations. No one will ever know the extent to which the urban middle class would actually have participated in a popular uprising if the Chun government had not caved in to opposition demands. In fact, following the reforms of 1987 and the direct election of a new president, most white-collar workers pulled back from their brief alliance with radical students and returned to normal middle-class preoccupations.

Until 1987 a distinctive feature of Korean society had been the lack of organized interest groups, except for commercial and industrial associations. The Park and Chun governments were unwilling to tolerate the existence of large, independent organizations, particularly those that might oppose existing policy on behalf of such groups as farmers, industrial workers, teachers, the urban poor, or the press. During some two-and-a-half decades of "hard" authoritarian government, only the students consistently challenged the former generals who ruled the country. Demonstrating students risked arrest, expulsion from school, blacklisting for jobs, and precipitous induction into the armed forces. The riot police became expert at containing student demonstrations without harming anyone, but many students were subjected to torture while undergoing interrogation after arrest. Since June 1987, in an atmosphere of relative freedom, there has been an explosion of organizational activity, particularly within the industrial labor movement, but extending to farmers and, somewhat surprisingly, to teachers and some white-collar workers as well. Labor has directly and forcefully challenged management with strikes and sit-ins, while farmers have also vigorously pressed their claims.

Koreans are celebrated for their obsessive concern with education, and in fact upward mobility is to a considerable extent dependent on educational qualifications. Another route to success does exist, however, in which individual merit and luck make up for lack of education. During the past 25 to 30 years petty commerce and very small-scale industry have led to economic security and higher status for a great many ambitious, hardworking people with relatively little schooling. Some of these self-made men, such as Lee Byung Chul, the founder of the Samsung conglomerate, acquired enormous fortunes. Possibly with the growth of giant corporate enterprise and the development of supermarkets and chain stores the number of such opportunities will decline, but so far, in contrast with the experience of many other developing countries, this sector of the South Korean economy has continued to thrive.

While social mobility has been extremely high for a generation or so, largely as a result of increased educational opportunities, rural-urban migration, and an expanding economy, there is now evidence that it may be slowing down. The outline of a more sharply stratified society is beginning to appear.

Rural Society

As recently as the early 1960s, two-thirds of the South Korean population was engaged in agriculture. Today farmers make up less than one-fourth of the total population. Except for the landless rural poor (perhaps 6 to 8 percent of the rural population), they are reasonably well fed, well clothed and well sheltered. The most prosperous 15 to 20 percent of the rural population are able to send their children to college, take sightseeing trips by bus or plane in the slack season, and own a small tractor or truck. More significantly, such farmers are investing a good part of their incomes in increased productivity through the purchase of agricultural chemicals, pumps, machinery, vehicles, and greenhouses. More than 95 percent of rural villages are electrified, and nearly every household has a television set. The houses of middle-income farmers are generally equipped with radios, electric fans, electric irons, electric rice cookers, wall clocks, and sewing machines. The well-to-do also have stereo sets, refrigerators, and washing machines. These conditions are evidence of the revolutionary transformation in both farm productivity and rural living standards that has taken place as a result of higher grain-price subsidies, increased availability of credit, more advanced agricultural technology, greater urban demand for food, and increased government investment in rural infrastructure. In 1971 the government vigorously implemented a comprehensive rural development program, the *saemaul undong* (new community movement), and during the next ten years farmers, through compulsory cooperative self-help projects, improved their houses, village roads, bridges, irrigation facilities, and other aspects of the local infrastructure.

The differences in income between "rich" and ordinary farmers should not be given too much weight sociologically. As a result of the 1949–50 land reform Korean farm villages are egalitarian communities compared to those in many other Asian countries. *All* farmers in South Korea are small farmers, and while absentee landlords do exist, they are usually relatives of farm families who have migrated to the city fairly recently. In any case such holdings are not large. While well-off farmers have more possessions than their neighbors and greater security, they are likely to work just as hard or harder, share the same general lifestyle, and participate intensively in the life of the community. They are closely bound to their fellow villagers by ties of kinship, neighborhood, and social responsibility. As a result of large-scale out-migration, whereby many of the poorest and richest households left for towns and cities, villages today are possibly even more cohesive and homogeneous than in the past.

In general the rural population tends to be politically conservative, but regional loyalty takes precedence over all other issues at election time. Hostilities between regions extend far back in Korean history; these are perpetuated in the intense rivalry between the Cholla provinces in the southwest and the Kyongsang provinces of the southeast.

Korean farmers are very high-cost producers in terms of international prices, and therefore (like Japanese farmers) their economic well-being depends on government price subsidies and restrictions on the importation of agricultural products from abroad. They are, therefore, particularly vulnerable to American insistence on exporting agricultural products to South Korea. After a decade of rapid improvement in living standards during the 1970s, the situation of farmers became more precarious in the 1980s. The cost of manufactured goods that they must buy from the industrial sector has increased disproportionately compared with price increases for their agricultural products. At the same time household debt has increased, in part because of rampant consumerism.

Currently the most severe threat to the farm economy comes from the decision of economists at the Economic Planning Board (EPB) to reduce grain price subsidies on the grounds that they are inflationary. But the EPB, while responsible for formulating national economic policy, is not the only agency involved. The farm population, although numbering fewer than 8 million, has disproportionate representation in the National Assembly, particularly among the opposition parties, and there are many high-ranking bureaucrats, particularly those in the Ministry of Agriculture and Forests and special advisers to the president, who feel strongly that farmers are an important source of social and political stability. Accordingly farm policy debates in Seoul tend to be bitter, infused as much with emotion as with economic rigor.

The Poor, Inequality, and Economic Injustice

Absolute poverty rates (the incidence of families with income below a certain fixed amount) have declined sharply with economic growth, from 23.4 percent in 1970, to 9.8 percent in 1980, to only 5.5 percent (or 2.3 million people in poverty) in 1988. The rates are roughly equal in rural and urban areas. People in this category, which comprises mainly the old, the sick, those with other disabilities, families without a male head of household, and in rural areas those without land, receive minimal "survival assistance" from the government. In terms of relative poverty, however, the Korea Development Institute (the most influential, government-funded, economic think tank) has estimated that between 20 and 30 percent of the population is unable to maintain a minimal, decent standard of living. (Households that spend less than 60 percent of the average urban household expenditure are considered to be in relative poverty.) Female-headed households make up 31 percent of poor households, and unemployment rates in such households are much higher than for the population as a whole. What employment there is tends to be as unskilled manual labor or in the lowest-paid factory jobs. According to a 1978 survey conducted by Seoul National University sociologist Hong Doo Seung, poor people did not at that time usually blame the system, believing either that they were unlucky or that they were personally responsible for their misfortune. After a decade of increasingly intense attacks on the political and economic structure by radical students and the media, however, attitudes may have changed. In any case throughout Korean society there is much greater concern for the poor than in the past, and President Roh's government is investing large amounts in more substantial welfare programs and low-income housing projects.

It appears that in contemporary South Korea concepts of social and economic justice as expressions of a more basic egalitarian ideal have become a pervasive part of popular culture. This is a reflection of the radicalization of political opposition to the establishment that occurred during the 1980s. A widely felt sense of relative deprivation is now a powerful social force for structural change. Although the interpretation of statistics on the distribution of wealth is difficult and controversial, most economists believe that, after a period of increasing inequality during the early 1980s, the situation is improving. But regardless of economic facts the social-psychological reality, or popular perception, is that the distribution of wealth is badly skewed and unjust. It is as if the frustration and resentment generated during 26 years of political repression were now being expressed, not just in the form of opposition to authority, but also in the form of extreme sensitivity to what is regarded as the unfair allocation of rewards.

Teachers resent the high wages paid to skilled industrial workers, whose educational qualifications are much lower than theirs. Workers in labor-intensive, low-tech industries resent the higher wages paid to those in the modern, capital-intensive sector. Women resent the higher wages paid to men for the same work, and blue-collar workers resent the higher white-collar salaries. Above all, perhaps, feelings of anger and frustrated envy have been created by continuing reports in the press and through rumors of the windfall profits made by middle- (perhaps mainly upper-middle-) class investors speculating in urban real estate and the stock market. Profits, particularly in real estate, have indeed been large. Because they lack both capital and information, members of the working class ordinarily do not have access to these opportunities. Also, critics tend to assume that some sort of collusion is normally involved in such investment schemes. In recent years the clamor raised about this and similar issues by students, intellectuals, the press, and the political opposition has been intense.

Labor-Management Relations: Toward a New Consensus?

The millions of young migrants to the cities (both male and female) who entered factories during the 1960s and 1970s passively accepted the fact that management's determined resistance to the formation of an effective labor movement was backed by governmental coercive force. Labor unions existed, but they had been established under official patronage and for the most part had little to do with improving wages or working conditions. During the period from 1962 to 1987, and particularly after 1971, there was no real collective bargaining, no effective grievance procedures, and no freedom to organize among the working rank and file. Progressive labor laws existed, but the government-sponsored Federation of Korean Trade Unions (FKTU) acted to contain the demands of labor rather than to promote them. If a dispute arose, or even if there was just an informal complaint, the manager could call in the police to make sure that production was not interrupted. Troublemakers were intimidated, warned, dismissed, and eventually arrested. After 1971 strikes were illegal, and management could invariably count on government help in settling disputes in its favor.

President Park was determined to prevent the rise of a genuine labor movement that might in any way challenge his monopoly on political authority. In order to promote export-driven, rapid economic growth his government made continuing efforts to keep wages low and preserve worker docility. Labor surpluses and high rates of urban unemployment in the 1960s and early 1970s also contributed to management's advantage in dealing with labor.

As the gross national product and living standards rose rapidly during the 1970s and 1980s, significant change occurred in the condition and attitudes of the labor force. An increasingly large percentage of young workers had been born or brought up in the city, and their educational levels were higher. There was a gradual shift from a surplus of labor to a scarcity, with an accompanying rise in wages, particularly in the modern industrial sector. Workers no longer compared their conditions and opportunities with those of subsistence peasants. Their expectations rose, and they began to contrast their status with that of other, better-rewarded members of society. In the densely packed cities it was impossible to ignore the ubiquitous explosion of middle-class affluence. Intellectuals, students, journalists, and other political opponents of the authoritarian regimes of Presidents Park and Chun increasingly emphasized the theme of labor exploitation, particularly in the 1980s. They continually asserted that the industrial labor force had for 20 years been sacrificed to promote economic growth and national prosperity, without having been allowed to obtain its fair share of the rewards. This message was, of course, eventually absorbed by workers, and their docile passivity changed to resentful discontent. After 1985, with the strengthening of overt student opposition to the Chun regime and in spite of intensified repression, there was a noticeable rise in the incidence of labor disputes and a broadening in the extent of labor militancy.

Along with the role of the government in suppressing labor-union activity, the development of a particular kind of management outlook and style in South Korea was also important. Because industrialization is so recent, factory owners have usually been self-made men who regarded the company and everything connected with it as their private property, subject to their own nearly absolute authority. Challenges to that authority by workers have been resisted with stubborn, outraged intensity. Although traditional entrepreneurs were likely to regard themselves as benevolent employers, there was never any question as to who would determine the firm's wages, hours, and working conditions. Traditional Korean emphasis on differences in personal status combined with elite prejudice against uneducated manual laborers to reinforce the factory owners' assumption of unquestioned authority. In the textile, shoe, and electronics industries, where semiskilled female labor predominates, discrimination against women was part of the pattern of exploitation.

The worker who protested company policy or who tried to organize a union was, from the owner's perspective, guilty not only of infringing on management's prerogatives but also of violating the rules of proper, moral interpersonal behavior. Employers still often tend to assume that labor agitation, rather than being justified by economic facts or by the workers' powerlessness, is really the result of infiltration of the work force by militant students or other leftist agents who then corrupt workers' minds with radical ideology. As a result of many years of unbroken industrial success, these ideas had by 1987 become deeply ingrained in management thinking. The anger, bitterness, and violence characteristic of labor strife during the last two-and-a-half years is in large part traceable to the distorted pattern of labor-management relations inherited from the Park and Chun regimes: authoritarian arrogance on the part of management and antagonistic resentment and distrust on the part of workers.

Now an entirely new system of labor union organization and labor-management relations is being hammered out through a series of violent and disorderly disputes, strikes, sit-ins, and lock-outs. The process, which is far from finished, is intricately connected to the political changes that are taking place as part of the transition to a more democratic system of government. New kinds of institutional mechanisms and procedures for settling disputes are being developed. Negotiators are painfully gaining experience. A great deal depends on the extent to which managers can change their traditional attitudes and convince workers that they can be trusted. A new generation of more professional managers is now replacing the original entrepreneurs, and there is the expectation that they will adopt more progressive attitudes.

Whenever there has been a significant relaxation of political constraints in South Korea, labor disputes have multiplied, most significantly in 1960–61 during the chaotic democratic period after the overthrow of President Rhee and in 1979–80 following the assassination of President Park. Similarly, after June 29, 1987, the number of disputes (most of which were strikes) skyrocketed, with 2,550 occurring during the month of August alone. In all of 1986 there had only been 276 such incidents. Nearly 2,000 disputes took place in 1988, and they are continuing to occur, though at a reduced rate. Many strikes were quickly settled, as employers everywhere made concessions to labor's new militancy. In a few cases, however, most notably at the Hyundai and Daewoo shipyards, strikes dragged on for months with accompanying violence and eventual intervention by the police.

Between June 1987 and the end of 1988 the government generally refrained from intervening in most labor disputes, and labor laws were revised in the fall of 1987 to remove some of the restrictions on union organization and collective bargaining. As a result, workers made important gains. Union membership has increased by more than 500,000 persons. More than 3,000 new unions have been formed, mainly in large plants that were formerly not unionized, and wages have risen over the past two-and-a-half years by an average of about 60 percent. Industrial wages today are as high as or higher than those in Taiwan, Singapore, or Hong Kong, a fact that has seriously compromised the competitiveness of Korean exports.

The rapid formation of new unions and intense collective bargaining activity have produced deep organizational and ideological divisions within the labor movement, however. The old, government-sponsored FKTU, after a slow initial period of adaptation to the new conditions after June 1987, has recently, and in sharp contrast to the past, taken an active and progressive stance, trying to promote workers' demands for higher wages, better working conditions, and shorter hours. Although unions at the company level that are associated with the FKTU remain to some degree tainted by their previous collaboration with owners and the authorities, they have the great advantage of an existing organizational structure. New FKTU leaders are trying to regain the trust of workers and attract new unions into the fold.

More radical, "democratic" (*minjung*) unions (mostly those established since June 1987) have proliferated and now have a membership of between 250,000 and 300,000 members. These unions comprise not only industrial workers but also some technical, clerical, and professional employees. In the case of such middle-class workers it is sometimes difficult to determine whether they are just getting on the bandwagon now that bargaining with one's employer has become fashionable and profitable or whether the popularity of the new unions reflects strong discontent and a more radical ideological perspective. Although public-school teachers and professors in publicly funded universities are explicitly prohibited by law from forming unions, they have nevertheless made determined, even heroic, efforts to organize. In the case of high-school teachers, their goal was to gain more control over the choice of textbooks and the content of the curriculum. The Ministry of Education has held firm, however, and there have been some arrests as well as dismissals on a fairly large scale. Most teachers who tried to form unions have been forced to recant in order to keep their jobs, but the issue of teachers' unions remains highly controversial and is unresolved.

Many of the new *minjung* unions are led by young activists with a revolutionary political agenda. For example, it is an article of faith for militant opponents of the establishment that nothing can really be done to improve the situation of labor without a complete restructuring of political and social institutions, the redistribution of property, and resolution of the issue of reunification with North Korea. Their goal is the establishment of a socialist or social-democratic state that will be completely free from the influence of American "imperialism" and world capitalism. In some cases demands on management by the new unions have been extreme, apparently directed more toward provoking conflict and disruption of the existing system than toward increasing workers' benefits. Because of widespread worker distrust of the old FKTU leadership, radical union leaders have attracted rank-and-file support with their policy of "strike first and bargain later" and their insistence that after years of enormous profits large firms can pay much higher wages.

Thus a bitter struggle is now under way within the labor movement between the FKTU and the *minjung* unions to attract the allegiance of organized workers. Activists are trying to "raise workers' consciousness" on political issues, while more traditional union leaders are emphasizing the need to construct a strong organizational base for collective bargaining. As of early 1990 it appeared that the *minjung* unions, after a period of great initial success in 1987 and 1988, were no longer attracting new members at the same pace as before. FKTU officials predict that workers will be more impressed in the long run by their unions' steady pragmatic concern with wages, hours, and working conditions than they will be by visions of political utopias.

Substantial changes have taken place at the Ministry of Labor, which has been upgraded in importance and now has responsibility for coordinating labor policy among the various ministries and agencies of the government. The situation with regard to laws, procedure, and authority remains somewhat confused, but government bureaucrats no longer take a consistently hard-line position in favor of management. On the other hand government spokesmen (and President Roh himself) made it clear in early 1990 that extremism and illegal violence, which they considered characteristic of *minjung* union militancy in 1989, would no longer be tolerated. Strong efforts have been made by the administration to prevent the formal inauguration of Chonnohyop, the federation of *minjung* unions, but the federation apparently continues to exist in a quasi-clandestine form.

In spite of the concessions made during the last two-and-a-half years, there is some question concerning the extent to which fundamental change has taken place in management attitudes. Some factory owners appear to be waiting for the current surge of union activity to subside so that the old system can be restored. They are reportedly pleading with the government to intervene on their behalf as in the past, and they have in many cases organized bands of *kusadae* ("save the firm" teams) to break strikes and harass union leaders.

Assuming that revolution is not imminent and that there will not be a return to the militaristic authoritarianism of the past either, there seem to be three possible lines of development for the South Korean labor movement. One, which can be termed the British model, would have labor unions associated with and represented by a political party that seeks to improve workers' benefits through public policy. A second, the American model, would have powerful unions that, under a more or less benign governmental neutrality, would go into battle against management on behalf of their membership. And, finally, South Korea's labor-management relations might move in a third direction—toward a Japanese model. This would involve the careful working out of a social and economic pact or contract between employees and management whereby workers are guaranteed fair treatment, a hearing for their grievances, a share in the firm's profits through wages and other benefits, and a voice in determining policy. In return they would agree to remain loyal to the firm, meeting prescribed standards of work effort, productivity, and quality control. This kind of accommodation requires a spirit of compromise, mutual trust, and confidence in the impartial operation of well-established and well-understood procedures that certainly does not exist on the Korean labor scene today. In fact, although Koreans are well aware of Japan's successes in this area, there is by no means a consensus that labor-management relations should move in such a direction.

The Student Movement

For many years, going back at least as far as the period of Japanese colonial rule, Korean students have self-consciously adopted the role of "national conscience," condemning current abuses and defining national goals and ideals. To a considerable extent the nation as a whole has concurred, granting students their position of uncontaminated moral leadership and heroic responsibility to fight evil. Large-scale, more or less spontaneous student demonstrations were instrumental in overthrowing the corrupt, inept, and autocratic rule of Syngman Rhee in 1960. Then, in 1979 and 1980, after the assassination of President Park, students demonstrated in massive numbers and with tragic results against Chun Doo Hwan's seizure of power. During the 26 years of militaristic, repressive government under Presidents Park and Chun, an increasingly well-organized student movement more or less continuously mobilized overt opposition to those in power on a wide variety of issues. Constantly demonstrating in the streets or at the university gates, students risked personal injury, arrest, jail sentences, and torture. Most South Koreans not only respected their dedication and courage but also recognized that the students represented the only significant force for political change during this period.

Although there have always been radical, leftist strands in student thought, the movement as a whole was until 1980 moderate and reformist in outlook. Its goal was to replace South Korean authoritarianism with a liberal democratic system modeled after that of the United States. The killing of large numbers of student demonstrators by special forces units in May 1980 in the southwestern city of Kwangju, however, proved to be an ideological watershed. As a result of this massacre, students were thoroughly disillusioned with continued American military, diplomatic, and economic support for the military dictatorship in South Korea, and they abandoned the idea of democratic reform as unrealistic. They no longer looked to the United States for help and inspiration. Instead they regarded Washington as part of the problem.

The student movement became more clandestine, more tightly organized, and much more radical during the first few years of Chun's regime. In accordance with their new ideological perspective, students called for a fundamental restructuring of Korean society that could only be accomplished by revolution. The United States was now regarded as the enemy, not only because it supported President Chun but also because of the conviction that Washington had engineered the division of the nation and imposed an anti-communist ideology on South Koreans in order to perpetuate it. An intensely emotional nationalistic fervor for reunification with North Korea became the core element of student thought.

Of a total college and university student population of more than 1.2 million, perhaps between 3 and 5 percent (about 50,000) were recruited and mobilized as militant student activists throughout the country. After 1984 the size and intensity of anti-government demonstrations steadily increased, accompanied by an intensification of revolutionary and anti-American invective. Another 5 to 10 percent of students were strongly sympathetic to the militant cause, even though they were not hard-core members, and a certain proportion of them could be counted on to join in once the emotional forces of a full-scale demonstration had been generated.

Before June 1987, most ordinary, middle-class Koreans regarded the student activists' ideological proclamations as too extreme, but they nevertheless supported the principal objective: to bring an end to

President Chun's rule. When this goal was finally accomplished in 1987–88 and initial steps toward democratization were implemented, students did not abandon their revolutionary mission. Insisting that the Roh Tae Woo government was simply a perpetuation of the previous regime without significant change, a smaller, more extremist student movement, using more violent tactics, intensified its opposition to the status quo. In recent years students have been deeply involved in labor agitation and the formation of *minjung* unions. They have pursued the goal of reconciliation with North Korea, and they have continued to denounce U.S. "imperialism." They now serve as a sort of fanatically activist vanguard for a new element in Korean society, the quasi-legitimate left.

But, by intensifying their extremism, student militants since 1987 appear to have increasingly separated themselves from mainstream opinion. For the first time moderate and conservative students are speaking out against the radicals, and a few cases of violent conflicts within university student councils have been reported. Until very recently such conflicts only took place between radical and still more radical factions within the movement. In 1988 the National Council of University Student Representatives (Chondaehyop), which is the overtly radical wing of the student movement, controlled nearly all the student councils of major Korean universities. In elections held in November 1989, however, Chondaehyop candidates were defeated at nearly half the universities, including the most prestigious and until now the most radical, Seoul National University. Events in Eastern Europe and the Soviet Union have had a profoundly disturbing effect on student thought, and the situation as of mid-1990 could best be described as one of intense ideological ferment. After ten years of increasingly leftist radicalization, mainstream student opinion seems to have shifted course, and there is now a great deal of talk of reform and a search for social-democratic solutions to current problems. Nevertheless, hard-core Stalinist elements remain within the movement, retaining both their commitment and their cohesive, disciplined organizational base. Members of these groups continue to advocate violent revolutionary struggle.

Students' espousal of North Korean propaganda themes and their campaign to promote reunification on North Korean terms has antagonized large segments of the population. And while the United States has become a convenient scapegoat for much contemporary dissatisfaction, many people nevertheless feel that the shrill denunciations of the United States by radical students go too far.

It would be a mistake, however, to assume that the student movement is completely isolated and without support. There are close links with progressive intellectuals, well-funded Christian groups, labor unions, some opposition politicians, and others who seek fundamental social and political change. And there is an increasingly large number of former student radicals who retain their ideological orientation after graduation. Even if many Koreans find student thought and actions impractical, dangerous, and personally repugnant, there is the continuing recognition that the motives are pure.

So far the movement has been unsuccessful in convincing Koreans that only revolutionary change can solve the country's most acute problems. Nor has it been able to prevent Roh Tae Woo from consolidating his position as a moderate president. And certainly radical student attitudes toward reconciliation with North Korea are widely believed to be dangerously naive. Nevertheless, in terms of their stated goal of raising the consciousness of the Korean people, student activists have been remarkably effective. Their alternative perspective on many issues has penetrated deeply into popular thinking in recent years, albeit in diluted form. They have successfully promoted anti-Americanism, and their insistence that the highest priority be given to reunification has helped prod the government into action. With regard to the treatment of industrial labor and the distribution of wealth, formerly subversive battle cries that were heard only in demonstrations at university gates have now become conventional wisdom. Student activists today exemplify a nationalistic and moralistic utopianism that has become an increasingly influential component in South Korean ideology.

Prospects

Can contemporary Korean society best be described in terms of cohesion and the potential for further integrated progress, or is it more realistic to emphasize its divisiveness and the potential for conflict? Today, certainly, the tensions, discontent, and strong voices of political dissent that were repressed for so long are being freely and exuberantly expressed. The process of correcting the distortions and injustices of the past is well under way. If, in the short run, this cacophony gives the impression that things are coming apart at the seams, perhaps the longer-term effect will be a positive one.

Any attempt to gauge South Korean prospects for orderly, harmonious development must place great weight on the desire of the large and growing middle class to preserve its gains and pursue its goals for the future. The explosive growth of the Christian church (more than 25 percent of all South Koreans are now practicing Christians) is probably also helping to bring about a more cohesive and uniform system of values. Progressive elements of the church (both Catholic and Protestant) are deeply involved in the radical movement, and there is a large and active ministry to the poor. But the church has probably had its greatest success as a kind of legitimizing, respectable faith for the new middle class. In any case Koreans take their religion seriously, and Christianity must be seen as a force for constructive integration rather than for division.

The year 1990 will probably be a year of slower economic growth, but there is no reason to expect a disastrous downturn. All the ingredients of the economic "miracle" remain in place: an educated, conscientious, and ambitious labor force; an ample supply of competent, hard-driving managers and entrepreneurs with access to investment capital; sophisticated engineers and scientists eager to adopt the latest technology; and a highly skilled technocratic administration with a superb track record of managing rapid growth.

In contrast to these stabilizing influences there is always the possibility that the discontent of well-organized and determined groups such as the militant students, labor, or the military will erupt with unpredictable and uncontrollable volatility. Continuity and fundamental structural change remain in a state of highly unstable tension. The current drive for greater social and economic justice confronts long-established privilege. A major security crisis, a worldwide depression, or greatly increased protectionist measures against South Korean exports could all have a disastrous impact on social stability.

Barring such catastrophes, however, the future looks reasonably secure. A substantial degree of consensus exists on national goals, and there is a very considerable degree of self-confidence regarding the ability to reach them. The family system is intact, and although crime rates are rising, they are still low by international standards. The current level of shrill divisiveness can be expected to moderate with the consolidation of effective democratic institutions, the development of a stable labor union system that has the confidence of its members, and a greater degree of official tolerance for leftist opinions and organizations. The formation of a pluralist state has been impeded during the modern period, both by authoritarian cultural traditions and by authoritarian governments. Now, in an increasingly cosmopolitan and democratic society, a balance must be found between the driving force of individualism and the continuing strength of collective, communitarian traditions.

6
On Native Grounds: Revolution and Renaissance in Art and Culture

Seong-Kon Kim

Most Koreans who experienced the 1980s will remember the decade as a period of dramatic upheaval and bewildering and seemingly chaotic change in their country. Politically, the decade began with a military coup that eventually brought about the Kwangju incident, in which hundreds of people were killed and thousands wounded fighting for democracy. It ended with a televised congressional hearing in 1989 in which the leader of that coup, who had been summoned from political asylum, testified before an angry audience. Socially, the decade began with the increased suppression of the press by the military junta and ended with the institution of freedom of speech and writing in a sweeping tide of democratization. The monochromatic military culture that characterized the beginning of the decade was by its end transformed into colorful diversity in every aspect of life.

The decade witnessed a series of astonishing events that could not have occurred previously: the anti-nuclear, women's liberation, and civil rights movements, workers' strikes, miners' sit-ins, farmers' rallies, teachers' picket lines, and students' anti-government demonstrations, among others. On nightly newscasts Koreans learned about the Miss Universe Pageant, the Asian Games, and the 1988 Olympics, all held in Seoul in the midst of social and political turmoil. It was a decade of possibility, a time when people were attracted to the ideals of liberation, liberalism, and democracy. Koreans were beginning to penetrate the mysteries of heretofore forbidden knowledge. There was frequent discussion and publication of Marxist books, which had been previously strictly prohibited. Some publishing companies even reprinted books that had been published in North Korea, creating a free market of ideology in South Korea for the first time in its history. These developments culminated in the complete Korean translation and marketing of Karl Marx's *Das Kapital* in 1987, a work that had been proscribed for the previous 42 years.

It was popular pressure that brought about these radical democratic transformations in South Korean society. This pressure first forced the government to issue the June 29, 1987, announcement that guaranteed all-out democratization. The powerful and persistent demand of the Korean people for democracy in the 1980s gave an impetus to revolution and reform and inspired people to combine the quest for social justice with the search for an awareness of each individual's relationship to the explosive social history of their nation. Not all Koreans participated in this idealistic search, however. Inevitably, there were those who, inspired only by the recent economic prosperity, sought materialistic pleasures and were motivated by greed. Although their numbers were small, their influence was considerable: materialism and hedonism came to pervade South Korean society, and there was a confrontation between those advocating instant gratification and those counseling patience and long-term planning.

Despite internal conflicts, South Korea emerged as an international economic power in the eighties. Once they felt secure economically and politically, Koreans began to recover their self-confidence and their cultural pride and identity, all of which had been seriously damaged by the massive influx of foreign influence since the Japanese occupation in 1910. One of the most remarkable characteristics of the eighties in South Korea was a new interest in the nation's cultural past. Koreans began seeking their national identity by uncovering and appreciating their rich cultural heritage. A particularly symbolic example of this was a surge in the number of archaeological excavations, which now reached an unprecedented level. Other disciplines responded to this nationwide movement as well, creating a renaissance of Korean culture.

Although the end of the decade saw many solid gains, doubts had already begun to surface about their long-term viability. Whatever the recent changes in the Korean social fabric may signify for the future, however, it is clear that the deep-rooted shifts of sensibility that occurred in the eighties have indelibly altered the entire moral and cultural terrain of Korean society. In this sense, the 1980s will remain a permanent point of reference for Koreans today, just as the 1960s are for Americans.

A Quest for Native Roots: Korean Music in Protest

Although changes in other arts also captured the spirit of the eighties and gave it expression, music was by far the most potent cultural product of the decade. When the students mounted their great surge of resistance against the authoritarian government, they expressed their anger and fury through protest songs. When the factories were closed down by strikes, workers also used protest songs to express their dismay and frustration. It was in the eighties that people began looking at songs as a subversive and disquieting assault on oppressive systems. For their part, the oppressors came to realize the potential of protest songs to organize and move the people with a contagious, almost electric appeal.

The creator of the forerunner of the modern Korean protest song is undisputedly Kim Min Gi, who wrote such well-known songs as "The Morning Dews," "Friends," "Song of an Old Soldier," and "Jesus Wearing a Golden Crown."[1] "The Morning Dews," a much-celebrated song in the seventies, was banned by the government for more than ten years, until 1987. Although Kim was silenced by a series of arrests and confinements, his songs continued to be sung on campuses and in the streets during demonstrations. After the ban on his songs was lifted, Kim returned as the leader of Songs of the Korean People, an organization sponsored by the *Han Kyore* (One People) newspaper, to find and compile the scattered or lost folk songs of Korea. In March 1990 Kim went to Manchuria to conduct research on folk songs sung by the Korean community there. Upon completion of his trip, he published a collection of Korean folk songs in book form entitled *Songs of the Korean People*.[2]

Although the people still liked Kim's songs and welcomed his return, they felt that the songs belonged to the innocent folk era of the past rather than to the tumultuous present. Folk music required no backup instruments, only a performer and an acoustic guitar; its hallmarks, which were embodied in the mellifluous voice of the singer, were purity, simplicity, and sincerity. But the new age demanded a different type of music—more complex, more aggressive, better suited to the increasingly complicated and violent reality of the eighties. In the American sixties, this demand was fulfilled by the evolution of folk music into rock, the move from Joan Baez to Bob Dylan. In the Korean eighties, however, it was satisfied by a shift from the folk song to the so-called movement song, which requires the audience to serve as performers and backup instruments simultaneously. These songs were marked by diversity, complexity, and authenticity. Move-

---

[1] Although the artistic works mentioned throughout this chapter are in Korean, their titles have been translated into English, except in cases when the English translation is inexact or awkward.

[2] Kim Min Gi, *Songs of the Korean People* (Seoul: Han Kyore, 1990). [In Korean]

ment songs were the expression of the disruption and disintegration of the late 1980s.

Not formally recorded on paper at first, campus movement songs were soon collected and published and rapidly spread to factories, mines, and other demonstration sites. Many types of songs have been classified as movement songs, including campus demonstration songs ("liberation" songs), gospel songs such as "We Shall Overcome," and traditional folk songs such as "Arirang." Integrating a multitude of diverse elements, a movement song was not simply a passive protest song; it inspired an energy to reform and revolt, creating a powerful solidarity against the oppressive forces of the dominant culture. The influence of movement songs was so remarkable that KBS-TV broadcast a special report on the subject entitled "The Sociology of Songs" on October 18, 1989.

The surging popularity of movement songs even affected the Korean classical music world. Since the early 20th century, classical music had been ensconced in ivory towers and concert halls, where it entertained the upper class and remained firmly apolitical. In the new, politically charged atmosphere of the eighties, the popularity of operas and orchestra concerts declined dramatically while the pop concert business boomed. To secure its audience, therefore, classical music attempted to affiliate itself with popular music. The scheduling of regular pop concerts by the Seoul City Orchestra and the KBS Symphony Orchestra was one example of this. The reconciliation of classical music with pop culminated in the October 1989 staging of concerts by Korea's two most famous pop singers, Yi Mi Ja and Patty Kim, at the King Sejong Cultural Center, a facility that had previously been reserved exclusively for classical concerts.

Another major change in the Korean music scene in the eighties was the emergence of an interest in national music. As Yi Kang Suk pointed out as early as 1977 in his essay "True Korean Music versus Quasi-Korean Music," Korean musicians and music critics now realized that Koreans needed to recover their cultural and national identity in music and in other areas of life.[3] A number of music critics now proposed the establishment of a national music movement that called for the independence of Korean music from the influence of Chinese, Japanese, and Western music.

This national music movement eventually resulted in the expression of a strong interest in North Korean music on the part of South Koreans. The performance and study of all North Korean music had been

---

[3] In *A Collection of Essays Dedicated to Dr. Chang Sa Hun* (Seoul: Korean National Music Society, 1977). [In Korean]

strictly banned by the South Korean government for several decades. As a result of popular pressure, the South Korean government in October 1988 lifted the ban on the music of 63 seemingly less political North Korean musicians, thus enabling the patchy history of Korean music to reclaim missing pages of North Korean music. New light was shed on the leftist music of social realism that had been composed between the liberation from Japanese colonial rule and the Korean War. The desire of South Korean musicians for an exchange of music between North and South Korea engendered the so-called unification music movement.

These movements for a national Korean music have not precluded the continued introduction into South Korea of music from throughout the world, including socialist countries. Foreign orchestras such as the Moscow Philharmonic Orchestra and the Leningrad Philharmonic Orchestra have recently visited South Korea. Thus Korean music is striving to maintain a balance between nationalism and internationalism—to be Korean and universal at the same time.

The Rise of People's Literature: Literature as Politics

As a result of the social and political crises that have taken place in Korea over the past few decades, there has been an ongoing debate on the role of literature in society—that is, between the merits of "pure" literature and those of literature "engagé." By the 1980s, however, the latter had effectively silenced the former with the powerful people's literature movement (*minjung munhak*), which advocated that literature be involved in the social and political issues of the day.

The concept of people's literature stemmed from the citizens' literature movement (*shimin munhak*). That earlier concept originated in an essay "On Citizens' Literature," by U.S.-educated literary critic and Seoul University professor of English Paik Nak Chung, which appeared in *Creative Writing and Criticism* in 1969. In this seminal essay Paik advocated a new literature by and for the citizens (that is, all those opposed to the rulers), whose mature spirit and new consciousness would vindicate the rights and ideals of their class versus those of the feudal, aristocratic ruling class. Inspired by the spirit of the citizen in the French Revolution, Paik called for literature that would enable citizens not only to resist political oppression but also to take the initiative in promoting human dignity and integrity in modern society. Paik's exhortations came as a stunning blow to those who had remained isolated and apathetic in the midst of social and political crisis.[4]

The citizens' literature movement gradually expanded in scope, eventually giving way to the national literature movement (*minjok munhak undong*) that was dominant in the seventies. The national literature movement inspired a quest for self-assertion, self-liberation, and self-fulfillment in defiance of the massive influx of foreign influence and interference that had manipulated and even altered every critical moment in Korean history. The resurgence of national literature paralleled an ongoing social and political movement, a new nationalism that had emerged to salve the wounded national pride of Korea and challenge the cultural and political imperialism of Japan and the West. In search of national identity, writers turned to traditional Korean folk culture, attempting to find confirmation of the sensitivity of the Korean mind on the one hand and the Korean spirit of resistance on the other. The movement advocated realism, populism, political engagement, and spiritual liberation.

It was during this period that people began questioning the validity of the entire written history of modern Korea, which some felt was tainted by a colonialist perspective. Canons were challenged and idols debunked; iconoclasm and revisionism were rampant. For instance, the much-acclaimed father figure of modern Korean literature, Yi Kwang Su, was openly criticized for his conformity and cooperation with Japan during the colonial period. It was in this atmosphere that such writers as Yom Sang Sop and Han Yong Un were rediscovered and reevaluated for their defiant realism, which was deeply rooted in resistance to the Japanese occupation. Poet Kim Su Yong was also among those who were much acclaimed during this period, despite what some described as "petit-bourgeois" traits found in his poems, such as self-indulgence and intellectual timidity. Yet Kim brilliantly captured the agonies and *Zeitgeist* of the postwar Korean society, its relentless analysis of the intellectual's struggle to overcome a sense of defeat and despair, impotence and futility. Soon he became a cult hero among college students, who widely chanted his poems, including "Blue Sky."

Important works produced by the national literature movement included Shin Kyong Nim's "Farmers' Dance" and Kim Chi Ha's "The Five Enemies" in poetry (Kim Chi Ha was arrested for this work and later released), Pang Yong Ung's *The Narrative of Punre* in fiction, and Paik Nak Chung's *National Literature and World Literature* in criticism.

---

[4] For further details see Paik Nak Chung, *National Literature and World Literature*, Vol. 1 (Seoul: Ch'angjak kwa Pip'yong Sa, 1978). [In Korean]

The national literature movement was soon incorporated into the broader people's literature movement, whose spiritual father is Paik Nak Chung. For the past two decades, Paik and his journal, *Creative Writing and Criticism*, have symbolized first national and then people's literature. The people's literature movement urged the populace at every level of society to assert its rights. It proposed that common people, not the elite ruling class, become the center of everything. As a result, a new type of historical novel emerged that threw light on the lives of such people, who had been largely ignored in favor of the privileged classes. As the movement realized its goals, conflicts between the privileged and underprivileged became inevitable.

As the people's literature developed, Korean writers came to realize that all the tragedies of Korea, including the recent military dictatorship, had their origins in the partition of the Korean peninsula by foreign powers after its liberation from Japanese colonial rule. Indeed, had it not been for the division of the country, there would have been no ideological feud between North and South, no separation of brothers and sisters, and no excuse for the dictators to oppress the people. These realizations led to a determination that literature must explore the nightmare landscape created by the post-World War II cold war ideology.

With the aid of the radical revisionism in history being advocated by younger historians who viewed the partition of Korea from a new perspective, Korean writers in the eighties began considering the meaning of their country's division and using it as a recurring theme in their fiction and poetry. The result was the emergence of the so-called literature of division. It attempted to delineate the intricate conspiracy of the foreign powers and the inadequate domestic policies that gave rise to the division of the country, which culminated in the Korean War (1950–53). Perhaps one of the most outstanding writers in this school is Kim Won Il. He believes that the division and the war have left a permanent scar on the Korean psyche, which remains haunted by its tragic history despite the country's recent economic prosperity. In his much-acclaimed novel *Winter Valley*, Kim brilliantly depicts the Koch'ang incident of February 1951, in which the entire village of Koch'ang, including women and children, was massacred on suspicion of colluding with communist guerrillas during the Korean War. In this novel Kim successfully captures the psychology of both the terrified villagers caught between left-wing and right-wing ideologies and the isolated communist guerrillas hiding in the outskirts of Koch'ang.

Another representative writer of the literature of division is Cho Chong Nae, whose ten-volume novel *The Taebaek Mountains* deals with the period between the liberation from Japan in 1945 and the Korean War. In it he effectively traces the process whereby sharecroppers became communists as a result of relentless exploitation by feudal landlords.[5] *The Taebaek Mountains* was epoch-making in the sense that it cast new light on the "other side" by narrating the story from the point of view of the leftist guerrillas, a perspective that had formerly been discouraged by censorship. This historical novel was serialized in *Modern Literature* from September 1983 to November 1989 and published by Han'gil Publishing Company.

Yi Mun Yol's much-acclaimed, highly controversial novel *The Age of Heroes* also belongs to the category of division literature. It portrays a man who becomes a socialist and voluntarily journeys to the North in search of his ideals. Because the protagonist ends up disillusioned with communist society, this novel was sharply criticized by the school of people's literature on ideological grounds. However, it is not an anti-communist novel but rather an anti-ideology novel, repudiating all dogmatic ideologies, whether capitalist or communist. Borrowing from the 18th-century Italian historian Giambattista Vico's notion of the Age of Heroes, Yi characterizes modern Korean history as an age of pseudo-heroes intoxicated with ideologies.

Perhaps the most dramatic event connected with the literature of division was Hwang Sok Yong's unauthorized visit to North Korea and his subsequent exile to West Germany in 1989. Hwang, a well-known member of the school of division literature, opted to remain in West Germany to finish writing up his North Korean experiences rather than return home to face certain arrest upon arrival. His earlier ten-volume historical novel, *Chang Kil-san*, which took him ten years to complete, is one of the most remarkable literary achievements of the decade. A roman-fleuve, or chronicle of a social group, it explores the world of 17th-century Korea, in which the common people revolted against the corrupt, incompetent *yangban* (aristocrat) class that exploited them ruthlessly. The title character, Chang Kil-san, was a leader of the people's revolt during the reign of King Sukchong, when the sacred ideology of Confucian ethics, the code of the ruling

---

[5] After the liberation from Japanese occupation, the Korean government, which was under U.S. military supervision, passed the Land Reform Act in 1949. Although originally designed to return the lands formerly taken away by the Japanese colonial government to their rightful owners, the act provided an excellent opportunity for a few members of the educated elite who had been pro-Japanese to become rich landlords. Farmers, mostly illiterate, lost their lands since they did not understand the complicated procedure and thus failed to file a claim before the deadline. Forced to become sharecroppers once again, farmers became frustrated and furious. These sharecroppers, who lived mostly in southwest Korea, were easily induced to become communists later.

class, was being challenged by the burgeoning secular philosophy of the common people, who defied the *yangban* class. In this novel, which is infused with a spirit of resistance against oppressors, Hwang brilliantly renders the landscape of 17th-century Korea and also presents a powerful indictment of contemporary Korea by juxtaposing the two periods. In another novel, *The Shadow of Arms*, based on his own experiences as a combat soldier in Vietnam in the sixties, Hwang explores the intricate conspiracy of Western imperialism in the Vietnam War. In 1989 Hwang was awarded the prestigious Manhae Literary Prize for this extraordinary work.

Another dramatic literary achievement of the eighties was Pak Kyong Ni's *The Land*, an epic novel that portrays the lives of the uprooted Korean exiles in Manchuria and their return to Korea to reclaim the land appropriated by the Japanese during the occupation. This roman-fleuve, though not dealing directly with the division of the country, explores its historical background by delineating people who are deprived of their land in the midst of social, political, and historical turmoil.

The ultimate aim of the literature of division was of course the unification of the country, or at least the unification of Korea's literary history. Until 1988 the South Korean government had prohibited not only all public discussion of North Korean writers but also any mention of them in Korean literary history. From the beginning, therefore, the literary history of Korea was limited, with students permitted to learn only one segment of it. South Korean scholars were not allowed access to materials on North Korean literature. Then, in the latter half of the 1980s, things started to change rapidly as Koreans began to demand the opening of the closed doors in their society. As a result, on March 31, 1988, the government lifted its ban on two important modernist poets who went to the North during the Korean War: Kim Ki Rim and Chong Chi Yong. On July 19, 1988, the ban on all literary works written by North Korean writers before the liberation was lifted. Soon there were discussions of these works, and research was being done on North Korean writers by noted South Korean literary critics. The publication in 1989 of *North Korean Writers*, edited by Kwon Yong Min, is evidence of the intensity of South Korean interest in North Korean literature at this time. Nearly all of the major literary journals published a special issue on North Korean literature in 1988 and 1989, and such issues sold extremely well.

The eighties also witnessed the emergence of workers' literature, which deals with the everyday lives of factory workers, construction workers, miners, and farmers and their struggles for survival. Decidedly Marxist, this school boldly exposed the exploitative nature of the capitalist economic system and encouraged the workers' resistance to it. The most celebrated leader of this muckraking school is Pak No Hae, whose real name and identity are not known. Said to be a construction worker, Pak's history of never making a public appearance has earned him the nickname "The Faceless Poet." His pen name, No Hae, stands for "workers' liberation" (*nodong-haebang*) and his primary aim is to inspire workers with class consciousness. Avowedly proletarian, Pak portrays helpless workers and farmers who are relentlessly exploited by capitalist society. *The Dawn of Workers*, a collection of his poems, is a powerful indictment of this society and a call for reform. Other prominent poets in this movement are Paek Mu San, Pak Yong Kon, Kim Hae Hwa, Kim Yong Taek, and Ko Chae Jong. Two journals, *Literature of Workers* and *Literature of Workers' Liberation*, are dedicated to this school of literature.

All of these schools fall into the broader category of people's literature, which was prevalent throughout the eighties. In the middle of the decade, however, a group of young radicals began criticizing Paik Nak Chung, the leader of the movement, and his colleague Ko Eun, a prominent poet and president of the Association for the Writers of National Literature, for their academic and intellectual tendencies. These extremists asserted that literature should serve as a strategy and tool to organize the people to do battle with the oppressive culture and the totalitarian regime.

Other literary critics, although sympathetic, perceived potential dangers in the stances of members of the people's literature school. Critics such as Kim U Chang and Yu Chong Ho persistently warned against the militant rigidity and exclusionism of the movement, asserting that these characteristics would lead it to make the same mistakes as the oppressive culture. Dogmatism and chauvinism may be anathema to Paik Nak Chung and Ko Eun; yet some of their disciples have shown a tendency to advocate questionable positions contrary to the wishes of their spiritual mentors. Today no one would deny either the epoch-making importance or the invaluable contribution of the people's literature to the republic of letters in Korea. But it can continue to be appreciated only if it learns to avoid self-righteousness and hostility toward those who do not subscribe to its ideology.

Against the Grain: The Audiovisual Arts in Revolt

Film

Film was not exempt from the radical changes experienced by Korean art and culture in the 1980s. Most notably, it was liberated from the censorship and registration requirements to which it had been subjected from its beginnings in 1919.[6] Starting in 1987, film companies were no longer required to register at the Ministry of Culture and Information and film scripts no longer had to be submitted for advance censorship. As a result, the film industry began to flourish in Korea. By 1989 there were more than 100 film production companies, nearly 400 small theaters, and hundreds of large theaters open in Korea. The same year, three Korean films received major international film awards: *Surrogate Mother* (Best Actress Award at the Venice Film Festival), *Aje Aje Para Aje*[7] (Best Actress Award at the Moscow Film Festival), and *Why Did Talma Go Eastward?* (Best Movie Award at the Locarno Film Festival).

In spite of this prosperity, however, Korean film suffered a major setback on another front. With UIP, an American film distribution company, now permitted to bring major Hollywood films directly into Korea, Korean films had to compete with them in the marketplace. Korean films were naturally no match for the high-budget Hollywood productions. To survive in this environment, Korean films had to become extremely commercial and heavily dependent on sex and violence, despite their serious themes and messages. Films of this type include *The Rainbow in Seoul* (1988), *Gypsy Mare* (1990), and *Prostitution II* (1990).

One of the most striking movements in Korean film in the eighties was the rise of anti-institutional movies and their challenge to Chungmuro, Korea's Hollywood, which was producing the highly commercial films referred to above. These new underground films, made mostly by young aspiring filmmakers, tended to depict the dark side of Korean life, such as the Kwangju incident, or the lives of the disinherited, such as factory workers, miners, and farmers. The makers of these films focused on marginal people who were excluded from the economic miracle, indicting the contradictions and inequities of Ko-

---

[6] Before 1987, producers who intended to make a film were required to file an application at the Ministry of Culture and Information by submitting the script for inspection. Later, they were also required to submit the complete film before its release to the censors.

[7] *Aje, Aje, Para Aje* is a phrase from a Buddhist prayer meaning, approximately, "Traveler, Traveler, Thou Who Leaves for Another World."

rean society and castigating the corruption and tyranny of the country's oppressive system of government. These new movies, variously referred to as open movies, independent movies, petit movies, and people's movies, gradually emerged from underground to compete openly with the Chungmuro films. The semicommercial prize-winning film *Talma* directed by Pae Yong Kyun, is one such work. When this underground film entered the mainstream, it was an immediate box-office hit, drawing an audience of 130,000 to the Seoul theater where it opened. Others were less fortunate; a young film-maker, Hong Ki Son, made a 16mm film on the Kwangju incident called *O, the Dreamland!* and was arrested on charges of releasing it without permission. Another young filmmaker, Pak Chong Won, who directed a 1989 film dealing with the lives of factory workers entitled *The Song of Kuro Factory Workers*, was forced to release it at a small repertory theater. By repudiating both the commercialism of Chung-muro and the censorship of the government, these defiant young directors revitalized the stagnant Korean film industry.

Another dynamic influence in film came from a group of young women filmmakers advocating defiant feminism, a movement that coincided with the powerful current of feminism that was sweeping South Korea. Over the previous 70 years of its history, Korean film had had only three female directors: Pak Nam Ok, Hong Un Won, and Hwang Hye Mi. All three were a part of the system, however, and thus differed from the new, radical feminist, anti-institutional women filmmakers. One of the key figures in this movement is Kim So Yong, who studied film in the United States. A recent project by Kim and her all-women team was a film entitled *Even a Little Grass Has a Name*. It portrays two women, one torn between her home and her job, the other an office worker who is harassed and discriminated against on the job. Through this academic and experimental film, Kim and her colleagues attempt to challenge not only the male patriarchy in Chungmuro but also all the oppressive social institutions and conventions in Korean society at large.

The only woman director active in Chungmuro in the late 1980s was Yi Mi Re, whose film *Yongshimi*, based on a comic book depicting adventures in the life of a vulnerable adolescent girl, was recently released and has been well received.

Advocates of independent filmmaking organized as the Association for Independent Movies of Korea on January 31, 1990. Among the remarkable achievements of this group are two video movies that are charged with social and political implications: *The Sangkye-dong Olympics* and *Korea Cannot Be Two*.

Television

Korean television became a mouthpiece for the government in 1980, when the military government took complete control of the stations by closing down privately owned TBC-TV and making MBC-TV semipublic. Recently, however, television in Korea has experienced a fundamental transformation similar to that of other cultural forms. The first sign of this change was a documentary, "Song of a Mother," that was televised by MBC-TV in 1989. It was a striking and powerful program that shed new light on aspects of the Kwangju incident that had been distorted and repressed for nearly ten years. The camera retraced vivid scenes of the tragic incident through the eyes of a mother whose son was killed during the fight for democracy. The documentary came as a stunning blow, both to the audience and to the producers at KBS-TV, a rival, government-controlled station, who soon produced a trilogy on the dark pages of the Fifth Republic.

Also in 1989, both Korean television broadcasting companies attempted to reflect on their past conduct and initiate radical reform. KBS-TV tried to revitalize itself by producing the types of programs that had formerly been discouraged, such as an account of the mothers of political prisoners entitled "A Place for Mother." Scriptwriters joined producers in this revolution. The writers were determined to challenge the notion that television drama equaled melodrama and that a love triangle was the only conceivable story. Inspired by a feeling of social and moral responsibility, they chose to explore the contradictions and conflicts of Korean society, often through the lives of the excluded, alienated, and disinherited. This democratization movement inevitably collided with the ideas of conservative board members of the company or government officials. And yet, young producers, scriptwriters, and announcers continued their fight to give expression to the spirit of resistance and democracy in the programs of KBS and MBC.

Tradition Versus Innovation: The Performing Arts in Transition

Drama

Korean drama in the eighties reflected the dazzling changes and tumultuous reality of contemporary society. In 1981, the law was amended so that permission was no longer required to open a theater. Previously, dramas in Korea had been staged in large, commercial theaters. Now, however, numerous little theaters were opened and a wide variety of drama was staged, including experimental plays. By 1989 there were about 30 active little theaters in Seoul, including the Echo Theatrical Company, the first of its kind in Korea.

Korean drama continued to be subjected to heavy government censorship until the late 1980s, however, and as a result there were constant clashes between the theatrical companies and the Committee of Performing Arts Ethics. In 1984 the committee suspended performances of *My Hometown Where I Used to Live*, staged by the Yonu Theatrical Company, for six months because of the play's political criticism, and in 1988 it closed *Prostitution*, performed by the Patanggol Theatrical Company, because of its overt sexual implications. But the tyranny of the committee did not last; as a result of pressure from the people, censorship was considerably reduced in 1989. Previously censored plays began to be staged, acclaimed, and awarded prizes. *The Toenail of General Oh* by Pak Cho Yol, for instance, which had been banned for 14 years because it dealt with the military, received several important awards as soon as it appeared on the stage.

As Korean drama savored its freedom from censorship, there emerged many dramas of social criticism and political satire. Some poignantly criticized political conspiracies; others boldly exposed the social maladies hidden beneath the veneer of economic prosperity. They attracted large audiences who were excited about this new freedom of expression, and as a result there came to be more Korean dramas than translated foreign dramas on stage in Taehangno, Seoul's equivalent of Broadway. During the decade, 643 dramas written by Korean playwrights were staged, with 1,200 performances taking place in 1989 alone. The most noteworthy event in the area of translated drama was the belated introduction to Korea of Bertolt Brecht, who had been banned for the previous four decades because of his socialist perspective. His *Threepenny Opera*, staged in 1988, and *A Man Is a Man*, staged in 1989, profoundly affected both Korean audiences and playwrights because they introduced the new techniques of interval music, narration, and episodic series. Most important, they provided a new view of reality.

Another important dramatic achievement in the eighties was the revival of *madangguk*, or yard theater, a genre designed to be staged in an open area outdoors for the entertainment of villagers. This traditional folk theater became a powerful medium of sociopolitical criticism by exposing the sufferings of the excluded and inspiring the people to reform and revolt. The *madangguk* presentations dealt chiefly with such sensitive political issues as the Kwangju incident, the division of the country, and the labor movement. In 1989 anti-

Americanism, anti-military rule, and the April 3 Cheju Revolt[8] became additional concerns of *madangguk*, which by that time had established itself firmly as an effective counterforce to institutional theater. The previous year, the First National *Madangguk* Festival was held in Seoul, with 18 *madangguk* theaters from nine major cities participating. At the festival, audiences were treated to standing-room-only performances of such works as *The May of Keum Hi* and *Kabo se, Kabo se.*[9] The former was a brilliant, intensely lyrical depiction of the Kwangju incident as seen by a girl whose brother was killed in it. The latter— nominally a historical account of a mid-19th-century revolution—was also a powerful, insightful criticism of contemporary Korean society. The second such festival was held in Seoul in 1989 at a time when anti-American feeling in Korea seemed to have reached its peak. Reflecting this, the second festival was more radical than the first, and its extreme ideological bias caused it to be received less enthusiastically than its predecessor.

Korean drama thus sought to regain its cultural identity and self-assurance in the eighties by returning to its beginnings in such genres as *madangguk, p'ansori,* and *taedong nori.*[10] Inspired by the powerful current of nationalism sweeping the Third World, Korean drama tried to shed the Western influences it had absorbed and develop a wholly Korean identity. One group of playwrights attempted to produce dramas based on Korean psychology and culture. Ch'oe In Hun, for example, wrote a number of modern plays that were deeply rooted in his country's folktales, oral narratives, and the ancient legends per-

[8] In 1948 there was a major proletarian revolt in Cheju Island. Judging that this was a communist-inspired insurgency, the Syngman Rhee administration ruthlessly subdued it, killing a huge number of the Cheju residents. Recently, there have been a number of attempts among younger historians to attach positive meanings to the April 3 Cheju Revolt.

[9] *The May of Keum Hi*: "Keum Hi" is a Korean girl's name and "May" refers to the Kwangju incident of May 1980. *Kabo se, Kabo se* (approximate translation, "Let's Revisit the Kabo Revolution"): In 1894, the year of *Kabo*, nationalist rebels attempted to oust encroaching foreign powers such as Japan, China, and Russia. The revolution failed when the king of the Choson dynasty asked for China's assistance. The presence of Chinese troops in Korea kindled the flame of the Sino-Japanese War, which eventually led to the Japanese occupation of Korea.

[10] *P'ansori* originated and developed in Cholla province, southwest Korea, in the 18th century. It was meant to be recited outdoors for the immediate audience by a professional entertainer who narrated stories to the rhythm of a drum. It is noteworthy that some classical Korean novels stemmed from *p'ansori. Taedong nori* (the Game of Great Unity) is designed to give the people a feeling of unity through their participation in a series of songs, dances, and games. Student festivals these days usually culminate in *taedong nori.*

formed in the traditional *t'alch'um* (masked dance) genre. O Tae Suk was another advocate of a new, uniquely Korean drama. Other playwrights explored the possibility of incorporating Western cultural influences into Korean drama. A series of international drama festivals held in Seoul during the eighties illustrates this point. In 1981 Korea hosted the fifth Third World Drama Festival in Seoul, in which 25 theatrical companies from 10 countries and 170 delegates from 30 countries participated. At this first international drama conference held in Korea, playwrights discussed the problems of excessive foreign influence on drama and explored the idea of a reconciliation of East and West in the context of drama. A Korean drama presented at the festival, *When the Spring Comes*, by Ch'oe In Hun and Yu Duk Hyong, was praised as embodying the achievement of harmony between East and West, ancient and modern, tradition and innovation.

The festival gave Korean drama international exposure. *What Are We Going to Be?*, performed at the festival by the Liberty Theatrical Company, was one of several works later invited for European performances. The Echo Theatrical Company's production of *Waiting for Godot* was invited to the Avignon Drama Festival in France and also to Dublin. And *p'ansori*, the Korean genre of song within drama, was selected as a research topic by the International Association for Dramatic Art in France. There were also international drama festivals in Seoul in 1986 and 1988.

Another advantage of these international festivals was that they gave Koreans exposure to foreign drama, including genres that had been unavailable up to this time. For instance, the shadow drama of Indonesia and the Japanese Noh drama were first seen in Korea at the 1981 festival. The Japanese Bunraku puppet theater was introduced in 1986 and Kabuki in 1988. In addition, dramas from Poland and Czechoslovakia were first performed in Korea at these festivals.

The Seoul Drama Festival, at which ten dramas were performed from August 25 to October 11, 1989, reflected the broadened horizons of Korean drama. As drama critic Yang Hye Sok pointed out in the Fall 1989 issue of *Art and Criticism*, the dramas presented at the festival were of two types: those that focused on the individual and those that focused on society. The latter type dealt with such issues as the effects of modernization and the division of the country.

Dance

Of all the performing arts, it was dance that changed the most dramatically during the 1980s, in both form and content. At the beginning of the decade, only 40 dance performances were staged annually; by 1989, however, this figure had risen tenfold, to 400. The increased number of performances engendered variety and openness in dance, and these became its hallmarks during the decade. The distinctions between ballet, modern Western dance, and traditional Korean dance became blurred, and performances consisting of combinations of the three were not uncommon.

A host of factors combined to bring Korean dance to this unprecedented prosperity. The dance departments that had first been established at Korean universities in 1963 were now coming of age. The little-theater movement of the early eighties provided ample opportunities for choreographers to stage their works. Also, such institutions as the National Dance Company, the National Ballet Company, and the Seoul Dance Company had reached maturity. Nevertheless, the decisive factor in the flowering of Korean dance seemed to be the secularization of art that resulted from the democratization of the nation in the eighties. The secularization of art did not constitute its vulgarization, however. Rather, art was liberated from the ivory tower and began to treat the everyday lives of the common people instead of the fantasies of the privileged class.

As was the case with drama, there emerged a strong interest in the cultural roots of Korean dance as opposed to a desire to blindly imitate modern Western dance. This resulted in the emergence of a new, innovative Korean dance that was charged with defiant realism and healthy nationalism. This new dance, variously called the national dance, the people's dance, the workers' dance, and the liberation dance, scorned the delicate, artistic, and modern choreography of conventional dance and instead pursued the dynamic, primordial, and primitive energy of ancient Korean dance.

Perhaps the most celebrated proponent of this new trend is Yi Ae Ju, professor of choreography at Seoul National University, who brought Korean dance from the stage into the streets. Dressed in white, the traditional color of mourning in Korea, she performed a requiem dance in the street at an open funeral ceremony for Yi Han Yol, a Yonsei University student killed by the shell of a tear-gas bomb during a 1987 demonstration. Yi Ae Ju often dances in public, mostly at demonstration sites, using the rhythm of traditional Korean music to help inspire the audience with the spirit of resistance and liberation.

The emergence of this radical dance in the eighties shocked traditional conservative Korean dance circles. Yet they were forced to acknowledge the refreshing vitality of this new form and the fact that it significantly broadened the horizons of conventional dance. With its dynamic energy and forceful movements, this new dance played an important role in the democratization of Korea. The liberation dance, for instance, was not only an expression of the intense desire of the people to be liberated from social and political oppression but also a defiant revolt against their oppressors. Indeed, every movement in the new dance was explosive and revolutionary, and each had a meaning and represented the fulfillment of a wish or desire. The audience was often invited to join in. One distinctive element of this new dance was, in fact, its negation of any distinction between the stage and the audience. As a result, it often forged the audience into a unified whole.

Boldly challenging the political conformity, intellectual timidity, and social frigidity of conventional dance, the new dance form attempted to create a space where art and reality could dance together, sometimes coming together in an embrace and sometimes keeping each other at a distance. It embodied the Korean spirit of resistance as well as the Korean people's acute sense of their history and their reality. Furthermore, its encouragement of audience participation reflected a Korean-style sense of community.

The Museum Versus the Street: Korean Painting in Crisis

In his review of Korean painting of the 1980s in the November 1989 issue of *Monthly Art*, Yi Jun pointed out that the Korean art world was at war. The battle in Korean painting was between modernism and realism, with postmodernism entering the arena later. Figuratively speaking, it was a fight between those who were attempting to protect museum art and those who were attempting to destroy it and establish a new form of art in the street. This battle was inevitable in that Korean painting had long been isolating itself from contemporary reality, the lives of the common people, and its cultural roots, remaining instead in the form of abstract fantasies confined to exclusive salons and strongly influenced by the West. As a result, those who subscribed to modernism or minimalism accommodated to the changing needs of the politically powerful—that is, they answered not to the demands of the people but to those of the elite. By so doing, they became the dominant culture.

In the eighties, however, a powerful counterculture movement called critical realism emerged to challenge modernism, the decaying dominant culture. At first, the resistance from conservative institutional artists was strong and tenacious. Yet the sweeping current of this new movement soon overcame moribund modernism. Its artists envisioned a world in which museums would be demolished, salons destroyed, and monuments dismantled. A new, nationalistic art flowered, which attempted to portray the lives of people in the street from a social, political, and historical perspective.

The first cry heralding the birth of this movement came in 1979, when a group of young artists calling itself Reality and Speech issued a revolutionary manifesto sharply criticizing contemporary Korean art, which it described as institutionalized and dogmatic. (Among the active members of this group was Pak Chae Dong, who went on to become a famous cartoonist and illustrator for the *Han Kyore* newspaper, established in 1988 with contributions from people disillusioned with commercial institutionalized journalism.) This new group, detaching itself from the mainstream of Korean art, explored the possibility of using critical realism to delineate the problems of urban life, rapid industrialization, and mass culture and society. Bringing art out from the closed chambers and cafes of the aristocrats to the streets of the common people, these young artists dominated Korean art in the early eighties.

Revolutionary and refreshing as it was, this group was soon criticized for its intellectual timidity and lack of revolutionary energy by a more radical group of artists who came to dominate the Korean art scene in the mid-eighties. These artists asserted that the leaders of the new artistic movement should be not the intellectuals but the people themselves. They maintained that the new art should portray the lives and struggles of the people in the most excruciating circumstances. They also insisted that Korean painting should concern itself more with its own cultural heritage and folk traditions than with Western paintings. The two groups behind this movement were Durong and the Citizens' Art School in Kwangju, both of which were established in 1983. Kim Pong Jun, one of this movement's outstanding artists, developed woodblock prints into an effective medium for representing the spirit of resistance and the lives of the common people. Art was now being produced for life's sake rather than for art's sake.

An even more radical group of artists emerged to dominate Korean art in the late eighties. They perceived art as a tool to serve a noble cause, such as people's liberation or workers' liberation. For these artists, the ultimate purpose of art was the enlightenment and indoctrination of the people. They made maximum use of the media of posters, banners, wall paintings, and street paintings. The most remarkable artistic achievements of this school were large paintings on draperies designed to hang from the top of tall buildings. The most celebrated painting of this type, entitled *The History of the People's Liberation Movements*, was hung at Hanyang University in Seoul. Unfortunately, the painter, Hong Song Dam, was arrested and imprisoned on charges of violating the national security law after he sent the painting to Pyongyang for display at an international gathering of student athletes. Such powerful nationalistic currents in art in the eighties eventually led to the rediscovery of neglected aspects of the Korean cultural heritage, such as shamanist folk drawings and mural paintings. This new focus on the colorful folk paintings of Korea was revolutionary because in the past only monochrome paintings in India ink had been treated as authentic Asian art.

Nevertheless, these artistic revolutionaries, after initially detaching themselves from the dominant culture and adopting an adversarial position, ultimately created a kind of new orthodoxy, no less tyrannical and self-righteous than the dominant culture they had originally denounced for those qualities. Discerning this ironic yet understandable problem, a new group of artists warned them of the potential dangers of extreme chauvinism and ultranationalism. The new group tried to reconcile tradition and innovation. In an essay that appeared in the October 1989 issue of *Monthly Art*, So Song Nok cited a new cultural movement called postmodernism as the third possibility in the arena where a hopeless battle between distorted modernism and militant realism had been raging for ten years.

The art critic O Kwang Su characterized Korean art in the eighties as the rise of an anti-imperialistic new nationalism, distinct from the militant ultranationalism of the past. Today Korean artists are still searching for the path to this new nationalism.

Conclusion

In the 1980s there was a serious confrontation between realism and modernism in virtually all cultural domains in South Korea. The conflict between these two movements provided Koreans with a rare opportunity to reflect on their place in world history and to restore their cultural identity and national pride. The new nationalistic movement that resulted from this conflict in culture brought unprecedented prosperity and dynamic development in every sphere of arts and letters by excavating and exploring Korea's rich cultural heritage.

Perhaps the most significant change occurring in Korean culture in 1989 was the gradual realization of the possible limits of the new movement. This realization coincided with the rise of interest in a postmodernist perspective that sought to reconcile the ancient with the modern and Eastern culture with Western culture.

Such a reconciliation may not be truly attainable, and the debate about it will continue. But even the dream of reconciliation is an important legacy bequeathed by the eighties to the nineties. In the spring of 1990, all the major journals and newspapers published special issues on the postmodernist perspective. Even the campus news-paper of Seoul National University, which has been in the vanguard of the radical movement, published a four-page special issue on the possibility of the postmodernist perspective making a cultural break-through in the nineties. Furthermore, *Creative Writing and Criticism,* the leading quarterly advocating people's literature, also recom-mended flexibility to the radical movement in its spring issue.

Since the late 1980s, Korea has seen impossible dreams realized in the Soviet Union, the People's Republic of China, and a number of East European countries, as well as at the Berlin Wall. At last Korea is beginning to change too. At the beginning of the decade South Korea was a stout, avowedly anti-communist country. Now, it has diplo-matic relationships with Poland, Hungary, and other East European countries and the Soviet Union. The People's Republic of China and North Korea are the only communist countries in which South Korea has neither an embassy nor a consulate.

In 1990 the Korean government founded its first Ministry of Culture and appointed the literary critic Yi O Yong as its first minister.[11] It is hoped that this will inspire another cultural renaissance in Korea and facilitate the achievement of harmony between the national culture and international civilization. Korea was once called the Hermit King-dom, but this epithet no longer applies. The battle between those who are trying to open the door and those who are trying to close it may continue for a while. But eventually all the doors of Korea will open wide and remain so.

---

[11] Until 1989 the Minister of Culture and Information administered all the cultural policies and events in Korea. Recently, however, there has been a growing consensus that Korea should have a separate ministry that deals exclusively with cultural affairs. In 1990 the Korean government finally launched the independent Ministry of Culture, a move applauded by writers and artists.

7
Korean Modernity: Change and Continuity

Michael C. Kalton

In East Asian tradition the Tao, or Way, of change is symbolized by a circle divided by an S-shaped curve so that the whole is composed of two perfectly interlocking dynamic teardrop shapes. One side is yang, blue with an orange dot in the middle; the other is yin, orange with a blue dot in the middle. Together, their shapes bespeak an alternating rhythm in which the peak of one is the beginning of the other. But the dots indicate that the complementarity of opposites is based ultimately on the presence of each in the other: there is no male that does not somehow include the female and no female without the male, no action that excludes rest and no rest that has not within it the root of activity.

As Korea has modernized and developed, the transformations it has undergone have followed this yin-yang pattern. The yang of change and innovation through massive exposure to and borrowing from Western and Japanese models has been balanced by the more quiet yin of continuity. The fundamental values, expectations, and patterns of conduct rooted in Korean tradition have remained potent and helped shape a distinctive East Asian and Korean modernity. Indeed, continuity and change in this case are premised upon one another: tradition without change dies and becomes a museum relic; change that cannot incorporate traditional roots will not last long.

Not every combination of tradition and change constitutes a successful blending of the dynamic and productive complementarity of the yin-yang pattern, however; failed modernization is a commonplace. The spectacular successes of, first, Japan, then South Korea, Taiwan, Hong Kong, and Singapore have all occurred within the East Asian cultural sphere. Why? Investigation of the Korean case will help identify some of the elements of East Asian tradition that have facilitated these successes.

The examination of continuity and change in contemporary Korea has a more immediate relevance as well. Although modernity has a common face and a common vocabulary throughout the world, in the context of cultural traditions these similarities become misleading. The glass and stainless steel of modern edifices, the components of computers and facsimile machines, and the nomenclature of political structures may be similar, but modern economic, political, and social institutions that are rooted in Korean soil do not necessarily function like their counterparts in the West. Understanding these cultural differences can help avoid potentially disastrous misunderstandings in international political and business interactions.

Traditional Korean society was shaped in important ways by a variety of forces, including shamanism, Buddhism, and Confucianism. Because Confucianism was the most instrumental in shaping the world of government, politics, and social relationships, it is important to identify the Confucian imprint on Korea's modernity. Indeed, premodern Korea is generally regarded as having been the most Confucian society of East Asia. The Choson dynasty (1392–1910) was the only East Asian regime founded under explicitly and exclusively Confucian auspices. When China fell under the influence of the "heterodox" Confucian school of Wang Yang-ming in the 16th century and then was taken over by the "barbarian" Manchus in the 17th century, Korea became the self-conscious bastion and preserver of "true" and orthodox Confucian civilization.

Thus Korean Confucian culture was marked by a distinctive degree of seriousness and intensity and was also predisposed to resist facile and pragmatic modification. These traits naturally did not make Korea's entry into the modern world easy—quite the contrary. At the dawn of the 20th century Korea was so weak economically and militarily that it was able to muster little effective resistance to Japanese imperialism, a failure that modern Koreans have commonly blamed on Confucian inflexibility and narrowness. There is much about modern Korea that draws on its Confucian heritage, however, and these elements have survived, despite vehement criticism, because they were so deeply embedded that their fundamental rightness remained a basic assumption.

The Confucian tradition arose in China in the sixth century BCE as a profound and systematic response to the problems of a disintegrating social order. Social and political concerns were at its very core, with the result that people were viewed primarily as social entities whose value lay in the quality of their relationships with others. In their search to restore order and coherence to society, Confucians assumed that, like any complex organic unity, society is endowed with an inherent structure. They conceptualized government primarily as the custodian of this natural order; its purpose was to foster and maintain it so that society could function harmoniously and fruitfully.

These assumptions, vastly different from the basic ideas that have informed the institutions of Western modernity, have continued to play an important role in shaping contemporary Korean society. Since many of the basic political, social, and economic institutions of modern Korea derive from Western models, this continuity with the Confucian past creates a complex situation. In spite of massive change and development, the Confucian imprint is still evident in the relatively nonindividualistic, nonsecular, and authoritarian nature of Korean society. These three characteristics and their manifestations within the context of a distinctive Korean modernity merit close examination.

Nonindividualistic Modernity

Confucians viewed society as an organically structured interdependent whole, of which individual persons are integral parts rather than independent units. Confucian education systematically inculcated its students with a high degree of awareness of this interdependence, teaching them that they do not originate and develop in isolation or sustain their livelihood independently. In this network of relationships, the highest value resides in making the appropriate reciprocation and responses—to parents, teachers, friends, and rulers. What is appropriate is determined by one's position or role in relation to others. Thus Confucian moral teaching is strongly role-specific, instilling not only a general human goodness but also the goodness of fathers and sons, husbands and wives, rulers and ministers, and elder and younger brothers when they properly fulfill their respective social roles.

The modern heritage of this mode of thought is a way of thinking in which one's role as a member of various kinds of social groups forms an integral part of one's identity. This strong role and group identification has proved beneficial in Korea today. Workers who have a ready sense of belonging and who identify with role expectations are highly productive. Similarly, it is possible for families and schools to imbue children with a strong motivation to succeed.

It is also useful to consider the perennial student protest movement in this light, for strong and differentiated role identities have made possible the routinization of a critical perspective and, at times, even violent protests of a sort that few societies can absorb. For years students have hurled Molotov cocktails in the streets while the Korean economy has steadily registered an amazing growth rate. During a time of intense student unrest Korea successfully prepared for and hosted that most taxing of international events, the Olympic Games. The violence that appeared on televised news programs in the United States as the Olympics approached was very real, the feelings deep and strong enough to produce periodic protest suicides among radical students. However, the violence was contained and coexisted with a remarkable stability.

Student protest in fact plays a useful and well-defined role in the polity of Korean society. The Confucian tradition viewed those involved in education as engaged in character formation above all and hence as a moral elite. The principal modern heirs to this tradition have been the students, who view themselves and are viewed by others as a morally pure and incorrupt voice in society. By their continuous critical protests, the students serve as the conscience of society and a necessary source of pressure for change.

Such conduct, often pursued at great personal risk and sacrifice, is also highly role-specific. Students from the most elite institutions constitute the vanguard of protest. Yet it is just these young people who, upon graduation, have proceeded to take their places in the premier institutions of the business and political world. The societal expectations for these roles are quite different, so the transition from the front lines of social protest to the bastions of conventional morality involves a change in role identity rather than a shift of conscience. The situation becomes unstable only when outrage reaches the point where it transcends accepted roles and others actively join the students, as in the 1980 Kwangju incident, when virtually the entire populace of the city joined the students in declaring the government illegitimate. For the most part, however, it is possible for the students to play the part of an active social conscience in a developing society and for their vociferous protests to be contained in a way that allows them to be a force for change without becoming disruptive.

These discrete role identities present a formidable barrier to those radical students who seek to join forces with workers and farmers. It seems unlikely that a limited congruence of specific interests, such as the students' moral concern with the exploitation of factory workers, will lead nonstudent groups to adopt with regularity the mode of moralistic activism associated with the role of students. If this were to take place it would be a cultural departure of revolutionary importance.

Strong role consciousness implies differentiation. Korean society remains highly structured and openly hierarchical even while allowing egalitarian ideas to serve as a critique of particular practices. Feminism, for example, is a powerful worldwide movement stemming from egalitarian ideals, but it is only partially effective in Korea. As a critique of distortions present in the highly patriarchal Confucian tradition it has been extremely effective at the theoretical level. Traditional views, for example that a woman must always follow a man's initiative, that submissiveness is the feminine ideal, or that upon marriage a wife becomes the virtual chattel of her husband's family, now elicit an angry response from many women. College students of both sexes cite such beliefs as evidence that the Confucian tradition is outmoded. Such critiques have helped women make strides toward legal equality with men, improved their access to education and jobs, and in general enhanced the degree of control they have over their lives and the amount of respect that they are accorded.

In Korean society, however, the acknowledgment of the existence of such issues does not constitute a challenge to do away with role differentiation completely, and the traditional sense of hierarchy has thus retained a secure base. The overall effect is an improvement of conditions within the general hierarchical framework rather than an egalitarian leveling of the hierarchical structure. This is typical of the limited but real impact of a broad range of rights issues. Greater autonomy for individuals and groups is very appealing in a closely articulated society where social control is a constant. Sons and daughters now often choose their own spouses, employees organize unions, and individuals and the media demand and increasingly are accorded the exercise of free speech. But such developments occur in a climate that remains highly sensitive to the existing social network and its claims. Individualism is widely identified as the ultimate danger of modernization, and social scientists and the media anxiously take readings and report on its advance, much as Americans do in the case of drug abuse and other social ills.

This generally high consciousness of one's life as determined by one's position in a complex of interdependent relationships makes Korea a networking society par excellence. Modernity has brought with it a greater degree of geographic, social, and economic mobility than ever before, but ties deriving from family, clan, region, and school are still of tremendous importance. Networks and skill in using them have important ramifications in business and politics. A Western-style egalitarian mentality is significant neither as a reality nor as an ideal, for all comers are not positioned equally in the network. Although economy and efficiency are important goals in business, in this kind of system they are achieved less by harsh competition than by sophisticated and finely tuned maneuvering.

In the political world, the importance accorded to relationships based on such factors as clan and region has long been problematic.

During the Choson dynasty it caused endemic and highly dysfunctional factionalism; more recently it has made the achievement of a viable system of party politics very difficult. In the recent presidential election, for example, the opposition missed a clear opportunity for victory by splitting its vote among three regional candidates. Compromise can be elusive when other ties and loyalties are so strong.

Indeed, although Western social science has used the pursuit of self-interest, both individual and private, as a primary category for analyzing and describing social behavior, the notion occupies at best an ambivalent place in the Korean political world. The Confucian tradition identified self-interest as the factor that, more than any other, could and would distort the proper function and integration of society. Instead, emphasis was placed on the fulfillment of one's role and duties in relation to others. In an interdependent network, attending to the interests of others is a way of insuring that one's own are taken care of. Such ideals, which may not exclude self-interest altogether, inform political rhetoric and play a significant role in public opinion.

In Korea the pursuit of self-interest is despised, an activity attributed to enemies, not friends. The residual negative feelings about Japan's colonial rule of Korea from 1910 to 1945 are reflected in the allegation by some Koreans that Japanese policy is always motivated by self-interest. Until recently, however, the public perception of the United States was rather different. Koreans frequently likened the U.S.-Korea relationship to that of elder and younger brother. According to Confucian tradition, the brother in the superior position in such a relationship takes care of the lesser brother, a "gracious favor" (*unhae*) that the junior partner is expected to repay with appropriate service when possible. Thus it was with almost a sense of moral relief that Koreans participated in the Vietnam War, a repayment for the *unhae* of U.S. assistance in the Korean War.

However, the Korean view of self-interest has contributed to the recent intensification of problems in the U.S.-Korea trade relationship. When the United States pushed its beef and cigarettes on a reluctant Korean market in 1987, the Korean public response to what they perceived as undisguised self-interest was a sense of betrayal and moral outrage that an American might find hard to comprehend. To Koreans, this was the move not of a benevolent elder brother but of a superior power concerned only with its own problems and interests—behavior characteristic of an entirely different kind of relationship.

A similar perception by Koreans is evident in the more active anti-Americanism of the radical students in recent times. Their anti-Americanism is frequently attributed to the fading memory of the Korean War, which they did not experience. Such emotional distance may be part of it, but *unhae* is not so easily forgotten in any event. The students have revised their memory of the war rather than forgotten it altogether, abandoning the elder brother image of the U.S. role in the conflict and instead interpreting it as just another example of the American pursuit of self-interest in its fight against communism. They support this view by quoting national interest arguments used by American politicians at the time.

A Nonsecular Society

Confucians traditionally did not subscribe to the concept of a personal God or to that of moral commandments. Rather, they viewed the universe as inherently endowed with an inner pattern that had absolute validity. This inner pattern, called the Tao (Korean: *To*), or Way, included everything from what today might be called the laws of nature to the normative pattern for human conduct and relationships. The Way needed no divine enforcement; just as the body naturally exacts a penalty for poor eating and rewards good nutrition, so the Way would exact a price for deviation at any level and reward its conscientious followers.

This way of looking at the world, fundamental to the Confucian tradition, remains part of modern Korean society. It still seems evident to Koreans that there is a natural and normative Way, even without an explicit Confucian label, and that intelligent human beings with good intentions will be able to recognize it. This pervasive assumption sharply distinguishes Korean society from secular American society.

Contemporary Korea's loss of an explicit Confucian identity has led to new developments. People no longer look to the writings and examples of ancient Confucian sages for sure guidance. Nonetheless the enervating accompaniments of Western secularity, such as relativism, alienation, and anomie, are not much in evidence either. On the contrary, value judgments and moral convictions come with a readiness that seems strange and naive to those more accustomed to the tenuousness of "private opinion." And while many are content with traditional values, others are ready to find truth in new guises: there is among Koreans a readiness for religious faith or ideological conviction that is much less common at equally educated levels of Western secular societies. This characteristic is clearly manifest in the almost unbelievable idealism of the students, whose youth and inexperience serve to intensify it. It is also evident in the cult of Kim Il Sung in North Korea, in the fervent anti-communism that has long characterized

South Korea, and in the unprecedented growth of a variety of Christian denominations in South Korea.

The extensive impact of nonsecularity on politics and government will be examined in the next section. This traditional cast of mind also has important ramifications for two aspects of Korean society that seem entirely new and distinctively modern: its business and consumer orientations.

The business and industrial sector of Korean society and the kind of material abundance its development has made possible constitute a marked departure from anything that could have been imagined on the basis of Korea's earlier traditions. Confucian economic theory was dogmatically agrarian, despising merchants and barely tolerating commerce as a legitimate activity. Nonetheless a tradition rich in complex bureaucratic organization and sophistication that shaped a disciplined society, placed a high value on education, and fostered a nonindividualistic self-identity has proved unexpectedly advantageous in terms of modern industrial development and productivity.

In the West the world of business and industry is the epitome of secularity. Liberated from the restraints of religiously imposed norms, it has had to rely mainly on contractual agreements drawn up, negotiated, and defended by legions of lawyers. In Korea the situation is rather different. In contrast to the egalitarian rule of law idealized in Western societies, the Confucian tradition emphasized personalized rule, minimizing law and applying it selectively and flexibly. Law was not so much a protector of rights as a punitive system to be invoked when more worthy human motivations and remedies broke down. A fully modern, Western-style system of law has been in place now for some decades, but to resort to law is still considered disagreeable. Of course, legal contracts have a place in the modern Korean business community. International dealings as well as large-scale commercial interactions in a more urbanized and less personal society make them imperative. But the strict adherence to the detailed contractual clauses and conditions demanded by the Western notion of honesty is alien to Koreans. A written document might betoken serious intent and sincerity, but to regard it as a detailed pattern to be scrupulously followed is an approach Koreans have had to learn painfully in order to accommodate the demands of the Western business community.

An approach more congenial to Koreans grows out of the Confucian emphasis on fidelity or trustworthiness in the relationship between friends. Instead of "honest" compliance with the objective terms of a contract, what is sought is sincere reliability in upholding and meeting the appropriate demands of a mutual business relationship. The appropriate demands cannot be exactly stipulated in a contract because the situations of the parties involved may change. A contract is a starting point, but what is expected is an ongoing process of negotiation and flexible adaptation based in mutual understanding. Trustworthiness, the moral quality involved, is measured not so much by adherence to the terms of the contract as by whether the relationship is properly maintained. This approach is congruent with the overall primacy of interpersonal relationships that permeates Korean society. Conformity to an abstract legal code and notions such as fairness carry proportionately less weight, as evidenced in recent disputes over copyrights and equal and open access to markets.

A complex problem associated with this highly interpersonal mode of operation and sense of duty is that it leads inevitably to the dependence of the business community on other groups. There is a common assumption that success beyond a certain ordinary level almost always involves corruption. In the complex web of interdependent dealings at higher levels, transactions take place that will not bear public scrutiny—the more so since giving and repaying favors (*unhae*) is the life-flow of interdependent relationships. Hence figures at the higher levels of society are vulnerable to hostile investigations; this makes them all the more dependent on the goodwill of others to preserve their political or financial standing. In such situations, government—the enforcer of law—has tremendous leverage to exact both financial support and cooperation from the business community.

Confucian sophistication in interpersonal relationships and the organization of networks may have contributed unexpectedly to Korea's modern economic success, but the materialistic values and orientation of Korea's recently developed "consumer society" are new. This development is consistent with the absence of teachings in Confucianism devaluing the good things in life and focusing instead on an otherworldly afterlife. But Confucianism dictated that material concerns be rigorously subordinated to the cultivation of moral character: overt concern for profit was considered despicable.

At first glance, it would seem that modernity has completely relaxed the tension between the pursuit of wealth and the ideal of moral cultivation. A tremendous national urge to live well materially has fueled what has become one of the hardest working and most productive societies in the world. There is a certain Confucian component insofar as the basic motivation is to achieve these things for one's family rather than for oneself. People often endure tremendous hardships to see that their children are well-educated and positioned for success. Also, when economic development became the overriding national goal, the accumulation of wealth could be, and was, publicly sanctioned as essentially a moral duty. Living well materially has been idealized in contemporary Korean society in the way that living well morally was idealized by Confucians, and the new middle and upper middle classes at times evince an almost naive enthusiasm for conspicuous consumption and material symbols of success. This transformation is not without its critics, however. Concern that material values are breaking down the sacred bonds of human relationships in families and in society at large is heard frequently—in the media, in political rhetoric, and in grumbling private conversations. But it seems to be more a reflection of lingering traditional values than the articulation of any kind of alternate agenda.

There is another more strident and focused voice, however, that of the radical students, who have recently widened their moral critique to include the business world and middle-class mores. Their critique is informed largely by Marxist ideas, a somewhat romanticized view of North Korea, and anti-Americanism. It extols the more authoritarian and less economically advanced society of North Korea as the guardian of the pristine purity of Korean culture, which the students contend is being corrupted in the South by self-centered materialistic values originating in a profiteering capitalist business establishment nurtured under the exploitative auspices of American capitalism.

It is unlikely that this critique from the students will turn South Korean society from its determined and energetic pursuit of living well materially. Nonetheless, as a critique of self-interested consumerism and the exploitative distortions introduced by an unrestrained pursuit of profit, it resonates with austere traditional values and hence may reverberate in Korean society more than one might expect. A kind of consciousness-raising seems to be taking place. A recent national poll indicates, for example, that disparity in the distribution of wealth has now become the top social concern of the Korean populace—this in spite of the fact that government figures indicate that Korea has been among the most successful societies in handling this problem.[1]

The Confucian tradition was never egalitarian, but it emphasized interdependence and cooperation and despised the profit motive as inherently divisive and self-centered. Some form of socialism rather than the aggressive capitalism of South Korea might appear to be the modern incarnation of these values. The world alignment that shaped the two Koreas into rather extreme representatives of competing social and economic philosophies is rapidly dissolving. But the experience of Eastern Europe provides a very uncertain model for what might develop on the Korean peninsula, because the antithetical rela-

---

[1] Tai Hwan Kwon, "Perceptions of the Quality of Life and Social Conflicts," *Korea Journal*, Vol. 29, no. 9 (September 1989), p. 14.

tionship of atheistic communism to Christian cultures is quite different from its relationship to cultures shaped by the nontheistic Confucian tradition. At the same time, the appeal of the material abundance provided by capitalism is beyond question, but its ultimate power is less self-evident in a nonsecular culture where new movements can draw on deeply rooted countervailing values.

Authoritarian Democracy

It is often remarked that modern Korean governments have been consistently authoritarian and that in many respects the society itself shares this characteristic. The commonly offered explanation for this is simply that it is somehow in keeping with Korea's premodern Confucian tradition. The government's oft-cited justification for continuing this authoritarian tradition, despite protests, is the threat from North Korea, but by now this sounds to many more like an excuse than a reason. If the road to democratic forms that suit South Korean society has been difficult to find, the reasons undoubtedly go deeper than mere habitual modes of response. One reason is that Koreans have envisioned a world that differs significantly from that assumed by Western democratic institutions.

A decisive development in the West was the separation of church and state. This entailed the creation of a private sphere, in which individuals had a "right" to their own morality, ideas, and religious beliefs. A secular government would maintain basic public order and serve as a neutral arbiter in the free contest of ideas and values for the private minds and hearts of the populace. This vision, articulated as early as the 17th century, has taken centuries to permeate the way people think and act. Confucian assumptions have been quite different. The Chinese character for "govern" literally means "to put in proper order." True order, as we have seen, is in accordance with the Tao, the inherent pattern, the structured and normative Way. Governance in a Confucian perspective was merely a matter of guiding and shaping society in line with the true Way. Insofar as that Way encompasses everything, there could be no *de jure* limit on the legitimate concern and authority of government, no private sector preserved for exclusive personal adjudication of ideas and values. The extent of intervention might be circumscribed by prudence and circumstances, but not by principle.

Modern Korean government has been caught between these two visions. The Korean constitution follows the Western pattern of separation of church and state, but this simply amounts to the allowance of basic liberties in the areas of what are conventionally recognized as "religious" beliefs. Meanwhile, the assumed Way, the nerve-center of traditional Confucian government, is permitted to function without limitation. Authority figures in government tend to assume that their role in ordering society includes seeing that the true and right way (Way) of thought and conduct prevails. If one assumes that the indubitably correct Way is readily discernible, this seems an eminently rational approach, all the more so insofar as wrongheaded and dangerous ideas, mistaken values, and depraved practices are so evident in the modern world.

Common government practice accords quite well with these assumptions. Problems regarding government treatment of political dissidents and freedom of speech attract the most attention, but there are numerous examples. In the 1970s "decadent" longhairs were subjected to forcible shearing, and in the 1980s raunchy foreign music was systematically censored. Key figures in business and education are treated to high-powered indoctrination retreats, and school textbooks have to be officially approved, with those that teach "correct" values and attitudes being written under close supervision. Government development initiatives are couched in moral rhetoric, and major campaigns for the moral purification of society are a recurrent phenomenon. Political discourse in South Korea is, generally, moral discourse, and, much as in the Confucian Choson dynasty, practical issues systematically become moral issues. This makes the process of compromise more difficult, for pragmatic concessions may easily be construed as compromises of principle.

As Western political ideals involving democratic rights and freedoms have taken on the proportions of an international moral crusade, this tradition of perceiving political discourse as moral discourse offers, ironically, a major avenue for change. In their Western form these ideals are closely related to an individualism and egalitarianism quite different from either the reality or the ideal of modern Korean society, but as an internationally recognized moral cause they have a tremendous impact in the highly moralistic milieu of South Korea. They provide a ready content for the moral critiques leveled by the opposition, intellectuals, and students. Democratic ideals are also an unavoidable component in the rhetoric of the government itself, however, and constitutional law must be framed to reflect this new political morality. Democratic ideals and human rights, then, have become included in the Way, the assumed normative pattern for the way things should be. Yet the government senses the implicit contradictions with its own sense of mission. Hence its tack is often twofold: it praises democratic ideals while stressing that they cannot be simply transplanted in their Western forms; rather, truly *Korean* democratic forms must be developed. Many accept this argument, for its truth seems self-evident. The students and the political opposition, on the other hand, continue to mount moral pressure on a government (and populace) more attuned to authority than rights. There is no simple resolution of the tensions between authoritarianism and freedom in Korea. The most likely result is either a relatively free form of authoritarianism or a relatively authoritarian form of freedom. The homogeneity and size of Korea support the continued assumption of a generally discernible Way, even though that Way now contains components of very diverse traditions. Indeed, the traditional Way itself included the yin-yang complementarity of opposites, and the yin-yang symbol is featured on the South Korean flag. Amid the clash of moral rhetoric, Korean society has a remarkable ability to handle such dualities in a manner that does not result in the either/or resolution of one-sided victory.

Conclusion

Traditional Confucian society in Korea was a highly structured network of interdependent relationships hierarchically organized and differentiated into specific roles, all governed by a normative Tao—the Way things are or should be. These traits are still manifest in South Korean society. In its flexibility, mobility, wealth, values, and expectations, modern Korea differs greatly from the Korea of premodern times, but there are lines of continuity with past cultural traditions that also differentiate it from the more individualistic, secular, and liberal society of the United States. In this respect, Korea exemplifies a distinctively East Asian form of modernity that has already displayed remarkable power in the economic realm. But it is not only the dynamics of the business world that merit our attention; interpersonal relationships, public rhetoric and values, and social and political movements likewise incorporate patterns that draw on past cultural traditions. To begin to understand the inner dynamic of South Korean society, we must look to the creative tension between yin and yang, tradition and modernity.

1989: A Chronology

January

1   In his annual New Year's message, President Kim Il Sung of North Korea proposes a "North-South Korea Political Consultative Conference of Leading Personalities" to discuss reunification. President Roh Tae Woo of South Korea is invited as the head of his political party rather than as head of state, along with other party presidents and dissident leaders.

6   Chung Ju Yung, founder and honorary chairman of the Hyundai Business Group, leaves for Moscow to discuss the possibility of joint development of Siberia by South Korea and the Soviet Union. During his week-long visit, Chung and Vladislav Malkevich, chairman of the Soviet Chamber of Commerce and Industry, agree to set up a South Korea–Soviet Union joint committee on economic cooperation. U.S. President-elect George Bush designates Donald Gregg as ambassador to South Korea.

8   The South Korean government provides heretofore unavailable publications from communist bloc countries to selected libraries for the public to read.

16   Kim Il Sung repeats the North Korean New Year's proposal for high-level political and military talks and suggests a working-level preliminary contact at Panmunjom on February 8. (On June 3, 1988, South Korea had proposed high-level political talks, but

the proposal stalled when North Korea insisted on the inclusion of military talks as well.) On January 23 Roh agrees to the preliminary contact.

17   In his New Year's press conference, Roh Tae Woo stresses his commitment to inter-Korea summit talks and his determination to deal with leftist forces in South Korea.

19   The South Korean Ministry of Finance announces that the government will lower tariffs, raise the value of the Korean won, and permit its citizens to purchase real estate overseas, all as part of an effort to curtail the current account surplus, curb inflation at home, and ease trade friction with the United States.

20   Chondaehyop (the National Council of University Student Representatives) announces its intention to participate in the 13th World Festival of Youth and Students (WFYS), to be held in Pyongyang in July. On December 7, 1988, a South Korean government spokesman had raised the possibility of dispatching students to the festival, but only Chondaehyop, a radical group, was invited by the (North) Korean Student Committee.

21   In South Korea, Chonminnyon (the Coalition for a National Democratic Movement) is formed. This co-alition of 20 dissident organizations calls for a grass-roots democratic movement and announces its determination to combat domestic dictatorships and foreign influences.

Police blockade the delegation of a dissident organization on its way to Panmunjom, where a preliminary meeting to discuss the establishment of a "pan-national conference" is to be held.

23   Hyundai's Chung Ju Yung travels to Pyongyang at the invitation of Ho Dam, chairman of the North Korean Committee for Peaceful Reunification of the

Fatherland. The Hyundai Business Group and the Soviet Chamber of Commerce and Industry exchange letters of interest concerning a joint venture for the development of Siberia.

Chonminnyon holds its first mass rally in Seoul, denouncing the Roh regime's "suppression of the 'people's movement.' " An estimated 10,000 people participate in the rally and the ensuing protests.

24 The South Korean National Red Cross Society proposes the convening of the 11th South-North Red Cross Talks in Pyongyang on March 28. North Korea rejects this proposal on February 15, asserting that the annual U.S.-South Korea military exercises (code named Team Spirit), scheduled for March 14, will create a hostile atmosphere.

26 The South Korean National Assembly's Special Committee on the Kwangju Democratization Movement subpoenas former presidents Chun Doo Hwan and Choi Kyu Hah to testify; both subpoenas are ignored.

30 A shipment of North Korean anthracite reaches the port of Inchon. The South Korean importer claims that the shipment originated in North Korea, while the North Korean authorities deny that such a transaction could have taken place.

February

1 South Korean Foreign Minister Choi Ho Joong and visiting Hungarian State Secretary for Foreign Affairs Gyula Horn sign a protocol upgrading their permanent missions to the ambassadorial level, making Hungary the first communist bloc country with which South Korea has established a full diplomatic relationship.

2 In Seoul, Hyundai's Chung Ju Yung announces the three issues on which his company has reached an understanding with North Korea: North Korea will

participate in joint South Korea–USSR projects to develop Siberia; a shipyard and a rolling stock plant will be built in Wonsan, North Korea; and North and South Korea will jointly develop resort facilities at North Korea's Mt. Kumgang.

4   At a press conference, the two dissident leaders Reverend Moon Ik Hwan and Paek Ki Wan announce their acceptance of North Korean President Kim Il Sung's proposal for an inter-Korean leadership-level political consultative meeting.

8   The first preliminary meeting for the South-North High-Level Talks is held at Panmunjom.

North Korea announces the postponement of the eighth preliminary meeting for the North-South Parliamentary Conference, scheduled for February 10, until after the Team Spirit exercises.

11   The South Korean cabinet approves a draft proposal for a "Special Law on Inter-Korea Exchanges and Cooperation." According to the terms of this proposal, the minister of the National Unification Board will be authorized to issue permits for South Koreans to visit North Korea. The Committee for the Promotion of Inter-Korea University Student Exchange, which is also supervised by the minister, announces its decision to send students to the World Festival of Youth and Students in Pyongyang.

13   Approximately 100 people are injured as some 15,000 farmers from around the country engage in violent demonstrations in front of the South Korean National Assembly building demanding the abolition of the irrigation tax and increased government purchase of red peppers.

17   The Heritage Foundation in Washington, D.C., is reported to have suggested that U.S. President Bush advise South Korea to be cautious in its ap-

proaches toward the Soviet Union. Bush schedules visits to China, Japan, and Korea.

21 The South Korean prime minister announces that Chung Ju Yung will be permitted to engage in the joint development with North Korea of resort facilities at Mt. Kumgang. Other proposed projects are rejected.

The United States is reported to be considering classifying South Korea as a Priority Foreign Country engaged in unfair trade practices under the terms of Section 301 of the Omnibus Trade Act.

25 Two defecting North Korean students arrive in Seoul from Prague, Czechoslovakia. Police block the Chonminnyon's attempts to hold anti-government rallies in 32 locations around the country.

27 President Bush, visiting Seoul on his way back to the United States from Beijing, affirms that the United States does not intend to withdraw its forces from Korea. The South Korean and U.S. leaders also discuss U.S.–South Korea trade and South Korea's policy toward North Korea.

28 A labor dispute at a Hyundai Heavy Engine Manufacturing plant in Ulsan, South Korea, is settled after a 67-day strike. Strikes at the Hyundai Heavy Industry plant there continue.

March

1 Police block a Chonminnyon delegation en route to Panmunjom, where a preliminary meeting for a "pan-national conference" is to be held between representatives of the Chonminnyon and the North Korean Committee for Peaceful Reunification of the Fatherland.

The Chonnongnyon (Coalition for a National Farmers' Movement) is organized and pledges to defend farmers' interests.

4   The leaders of the three South Korean opposition parties (Kim Dae Jung of the Party for Peace and Democracy, Kim Young Sam of the Reunification Democratic Party, and Kim Jong Pil of the New Democratic Republican Party) agree that the interim appraisal of the Roh regime should be delayed until President Roh implements democratic reforms and eradicates the legacy of the Fifth Republic of former president Chun. Roh had promised his opponents this interim appraisal at the time of his December 1987 electoral campaign.

7   Kim Hyun Hee, the North Korean accused of planting explosives on Korean Air Lines Flight 858 on November 29, 1987, is brought to trial.

9   The North-South Sports Talks are held at Panmunjom to discuss the establishment of a united Korean team for the 1990 Asian Games, to be held in Beijing. The two sides agree on the use of "Arirang," a traditional Korean folk song, as the team's anthem.

13   The South Korean Committee for the Promotion of Inter-Korea University Student Exchange proposes to North Korea that a meeting be held to discuss the participation of South Korean students in the Pyongyang festival. (On March 15 North Korea announces its agreement to such participation, provided that the South Korean government agrees to a working-level meeting between the [North] Korean Student Committee and the National Council of University Student Representatives [Chondaehyop] on March 16.)

14   The 14th annual South Korea–U.S. joint military exercises, "Team Spirit '89," begin. (The exercises continue until March 23.)

15   For the first time in the history of South Korea, the Supreme Court nullifies election results. The April 1988 results from the Tonghae electoral district are at issue.

16 Police block a Chondaehyop delegation on its way to Panmunjom. The radical student group was to hold a working-level meeting with the (North) Korean Student Committee.

The labor union of the state-run Seoul Metropolitan Subway Corporation decides to go on strike.

19 Eleven dissident organizations, including Chonminnyon and Chondaehyop, hold a mass rally in Seoul to denounce the Roh regime and launch a nationwide campaign declaring "non-confidence in the president."

20 President Roh announces the indefinite postponement of the interim appraisal, in order to "avoid political confrontation that would lead to extreme chaos." The appraisal was to have taken the form of a plebiscite, or national vote of confidence.

21 Members of Chondaehyop and other dissident groups join the strikers at the Hyundai Heavy Industry plant in Ulsan; the strike began in December 1988.

25 Reverend Moon Ik Hwan, adviser to Chonminnyon, arrives in Pyongyang.

27 Police block and arrest a South Korean National Council of Writers delegation en route to Panmunjom, where it had intended to hold a meeting with the (North) Korean Writers' Alliance.

28 The second session of the North-South Sports Talks is held. Agreement is reached on the official flag of the united Korea team that is to participate in the 1990 Asian Games in Beijing.

President Roh consolidates his position in the army by reshuffling appointments of general officers.

29 The South Korean government and the ruling Democratic Justice Party decide not to modify the National Security Law.

30   The South Korean government mobilizes some 10,000 riot police to forcibly disperse the strikers at the Hyundai Heavy Industry plant in Ulsan.

April

2   Reverend Moon Ik Hwan and Chairman Ho Dam of the Committee for Peaceful Reunification of the Fatherland issue a nine-point joint communiqué in Pyongyang.

3   The Soviet Chamber of Commerce and Industry opens a trade office in Seoul.

The South Korean government establishes a Joint Public Security Investigation Headquarters to investigate the leftist movements of dissident organizations. The government and the ruling DJP are reported to be contemplating a constitutional revision that would install a cabinet system of government before 1992.

4   The South Korean minister of justice announces that unauthorized contacts with North Korea by South Koreans will be punished as violations of Article 8 of the National Security Law, "Meeting and Communication."

8   The South Korean government announces a three-year (1989–91) plan to open its country's markets to foreign trade. The import liberalization ratio for farm, livestock, and forestry and fishery products is to be raised from the present level of 71.9 percent to 84.9 percent by 1992 in an effort to avoid possible U.S. classification of South Korea as a Priority Foreign Country under the terms of Section 301 of the Omnibus Trade Act.

13   On his return to South Korea, Reverend Moon is arrested on charges of violating the National Security Law. On October 5, the Seoul District Criminal Court sentences him to ten years in prison.

15   President Kim Young Sam of the Reunification Democratic Party publicly apologizes for the unlawful conduct of his party's candidate in the Tonghae election. The party's secretary-general is arrested April 20 in this connection.

25   The General Agreement on Tariffs and Trade (GATT) rules that South Korea must present a timetable for phasing out import restrictions on beef.

28   Police blockade the road to Panmunjom as members of Chondaehyop announce their intention to meet with representatives of the (North) Korean Students Committee there. North Korea invites 55 South Koreans to be "honored guests" at the Pyongyang festival. The National Unification Board declares the invitation an attempt to cause discord in South Korea.

30   Police block an attempt to hold a mass rally at Seoul's Yoido Plaza to celebrate the 100th May Day.

May

1   The Ministry of Education temporarily shuts down Seoul Teacher's College, which has been plagued by student sit-ins since a student committed suicide on campus by setting himself on fire on April 10. (The university reopens July 3.)

2   South Korea and the United States agree that the headquarters of the Eighth U.S. Army and the U.S.–Korea Combined Command will be moved out of metropolitan Seoul by the mid-1990s.

3   Seven policemen are killed in a fire at Dongui University in Pusan. Five of them had been held hostage by student protesters who set fire to the library building to thwart a police rescue operation.

President Roh warns that he may have to resort to special measures, i.e., martial law, if violence and illegal activities threaten the future of the state.

6   Two defecting North Korean students who had been studying in Poland arrive in Seoul.

10   A Chosun University student, Lee Chul Kyu, is found dead in a reservoir near Kwangju. He had been wanted by the police for publishing an article in his university's student newspaper alleging that the Korean War was a "national liberation war."

11   South Korean Deputy Prime Minister Cho Soon tells the National Assembly that the government will soon introduce legislation designed to curtail speculative investment in land. The legislation is passed on December 19.

18   An estimated 120,000 people participate in a rally held in Kwangju to commemorate those killed during the Kwangju incident of May 1980.

19   The U.S.-Korea trade conference in Washington concludes that South Korea will not be designated a Priority Foreign Country. South Korea agrees to further open its agricultural market and relax controls on the investment of foreign capital.

20   The road to Panmunjom is blockaded to prevent the meeting of radical South Korean students with representatives of North Korean student organizations. The students were to have discussed South Korean participation in the forthcoming World Festival of Youth and Students.

27   The Supreme Court nullifies the April 1988 election of the national assemblyman from Seoul's Yongdungpo-B electoral district.

28   The National Teachers' Union (Chongyojo) is organized but banned by the South Korean government on the grounds that existing laws prohibit such a union. The union calls for drastic reforms in curriculum and more democratic organization in the schools.

June

1   An estimated 4,000 students and others demonstrate in Kwangju to protest the May 30 government report ruling Lee Chul Kyu's death accidental
(see May 10). The protestors allege that the police
were responsible for his death.

2   Democratic Justice Party (DJP) Chairman Park Jun
Kyu reveals that his party is seriously considering
the revision of the constitution to provide for a parliamentary cabinet form of government. On July 5,
during a visit to Canada, Park again alludes to this
possibility.

5   South Korean Catholic priest Moon Kyu Hyun (not
to be confused with Reverend Moon Ik Hwan) arrives secretly in Pyongyang for a 14-day visit.

On July 25 the Catholic Priests' Association for Justice, a dissident organization, dispatches Father
Moon from Japan to Pyongyang to escort Chondaehyop representative Im Su Kyong back to South
Korea via Panmunjom.

6   On a nine-day visit to Moscow, the opposition RDP
president Kim Young Sam meets with Ho Dam,
chairman of the Committee for Peaceful Reunification of the Fatherland. Ho invites Kim to visit
Pyongyang and is refused.

8   Fearing national chaos, President Roh makes it clear
that he will not allow an interim appraisal of his
performance in office. His term is to expire in February 1993.

10   The South Korean government mobilizes 24,000 police officers to blockade a conference of representatives from six North and South Korean organizations.

12   In a presidential decree, South Korea's National
Unification Board announces "basic guidelines for

inter-Korea exchanges and cooperation." According to these guidelines, South Koreans wishing to visit North Korea must be recognized by the minister of the Unification Board four weeks in advance. This decree is the first legislative expression of the government's "single-channel" logic, which stipulates that any South-North exchange must have government approval.

19   The South Korean Joint Public Security Investigation Headquarters is dismantled. During the 77 days of its existence, 31 dissidents have been prosecuted in connection with voluntary contacts with the North, labor disputes, and violent demonstrations.

20   The South Korean government issues its final decision that it will not permit any university students to participate in the 13th World Festival of Youth and Students.

21   Im Su Kyong, a senior at Hankook University of Foreign Studies, secretly leaves Seoul to represent Chondaehyop at the Pyongyang World Festival of Youth and Students.

27   Representative Suh Kyong Won of the opposition Party for Peace and Democracy (PPD) is arrested for allegedly violating the National Security Law by secretly visiting Pyongyang in 1988. (The Seoul District Criminal Court sentences him to a 15-year prison term on December 20.) On May 28, PPD's president, Kim Dae Jung, issues a public apology concerning the matter.

A settlement is reached in a month-long labor dispute at Daewoo Shipbuilding and Heavy Machinery Ltd, in Koje, South Kyongsang Province. The dispute had been aggravated by the May 29 suicide of a laborer who set himself afire.

30   Im Su Kyong arrives in Pyongyang, becoming the first nondefecting South Korean student to enter North Korea voluntarily since the Korean War.

July

1   The 13th World Festival of Youth and Students begins in Pyongyang under the slogan, "For anti-imperialist solidarity, peace, and friendship." It ends on July 18.

4   South Korean National Unification Minister Lee Hong Koo announces that his government will postpone various inter-Korea talks for a considerable length of time.

7   As Chondaehyop representative in Pyongyang, Im Su Kyong issues a joint communiqué with the chair of the (North) Korean Student Committee concerning the independent and peaceful reunification of the Korean peninsula.

9   Over 15,000 members of Chongyojo (the National Teachers' Union) rally in Seoul to demand government approval of their organization.

17   The Agency for National Security Planning announces that Representative Suh received US$85,000 and 34,100 German marks on a total of 14 occasions in the form of an "operation fund." According to the announcement, the fund was allegedly used to finance the Catholic Farmers' Association and other dissident groups and the 1988 parliamentary election campaign.

20   For the first time since the issuance of basic guidelines for South-North exchanges the previous month, the Committee for Promotion of Inter-Korea Exchanges and Cooperation, presided over by the National Unification Board, issues a permit for a clergyman living in Japan, Moon Kyu Hyun, to visit North Korea.

24   Chung Ju Yung leaves for the USSR leading a 31-member delegation that plans to hold meetings concerning business cooperation and development of Siberia. They return on August 2.

25   Father Moon and Im Su Kyong leave Pyongyang for Seoul.

27   Seventy-two people are killed when a Korean Air Lines DC-10 crashes at Tripoli Airport in Libya.

Im's attempt to return to Seoul via Panmunjom is thwarted by a South Korean blockade.

29   Accompanied by his wife, a Chinese army major who is a member of the Chinese delegation to the Korean Military Armistice Commission in Panmunjom crosses the Military Demarcation Line, seeking political asylum.

31   Independent Representative Park Chan Jong and Representative Lee Chul send President Roh and Prime Minister Kang Young Hoon a letter asking if it is true that then-presidential aide Park Chul Un and others secretly visited Pyongyang during the 13th WFYS, and, if so, whether President Roh had sanctioned the visit. On August 5, the prime minister denies that the visit took place.

August

2   The opposition PPD president Kim Dae Jung and former vice-president Moon Dong Hwan are detained by National Security Planning Agency investigators and released the following day after 20 hours of questioning in connection with Representative Suh's unauthorized trip to Pyongyang and other allegations.

9   North Korea proposes that the third North-South Sports Talks be held, but the following day South Korea announces its intention to postpone the talks indefinitely.

12   Asserting that the government is utilizing the National Security Law to repress the democratization process, approximately 1,600 members of the South Korean National Council of University Professors for Democratization urge the government to stop such "political maneuvering."

15   Im Su Kyong returns to South Korea after a 46-day visit to North Korea. She is accompanied by Father Moon Kyu Hyun.

18   The ruling DJP candidate is victorious in a new election in Seoul's Yongdungpo-B district.

19   A Korean Air Lines Boeing 727 charter flight carrying 148 passengers, including a 55-member team scheduled to compete in the Asian Handball Championship in Beijing, arrives in Shanghai, marking the first landing of a South Korean airliner in China.

25   Kim Dae Jung is indicted without physical restraint on charges of violating the Failure to Inform clause of the National Security Law and the Foreign Exchange Management Law. (He had been booked on August 12 on suspicion of receiving US$10,000 from Representative Suh, who was arrested for allegedly spying for Pyongyang.)

30   President Roh reshuffles the major posts of his Democratic Justice Party (DJP), appointing Representative Lee Choon Koo, former chief of the party's 13th presidential campaign headquarters, as secretary-general of the party, and Representative Lee Han Dong as floor leader.

31   The South Korean Ministry of Construction announces that the Dong-Ah Construction Industrial Company has won a contract worth US$5.3 billion for a Libyan waterway project.

September

1   The South Korean Ministry of Commerce and Industry reports that the August trade deficit eliminated the January–July surplus, putting the nations's trade account in the red.

10   Three North Koreans, two soldiers and a civilian nurse, defect to South Korea by walking through a mine field and swimming across a river on the border.

11   In an address to the National Assembly, President Roh announces a new unification formula that calls for the establishment of a commonwealth to link South and North Korea at an interim stage prior to complete unification. According to the formula, a council of presidents or chief executives from both Koreas would be the commonwealth's highest decision-making body, supported by a council of ministers consisting of delegates from both governments. In a meeting with Commerce and Industry Minister Han Seung Soo in Seoul, U.S. Secretary of Commerce Robert Mosbacher demands that South Korea's value-added network market be opened at an early date. It is reported that the South Korean communications market will be opened in 1992.

18   The South Korean defense minister tells the National Assembly that the estimated amount of South Korea's direct and indirect support of U.S. forces in Korea totaled US$2.2 billion in fiscal 1988.

19   The South Korean defense minister reports to the National Assembly that the government has decided to participate, beginning in 1990, in the biennial U.S.-led Pacific Rim naval exercise.

U.S. Vice President Dan Quayle arrives in Seoul for a three-day visit.

24 Rallies against the South Korean government's suppression of Chonkyocho are held in 12 cities, with an estimated 40,000 people participating.

25 For the first time since the end of World War II, Koreans residing in the Soviet Union visit South Korea. The visitors participate in the first pannational ethnic Korean sports festival, which is held in Seoul from September 26 to 30.

The central committee of the Chonminnyon, the Coalition for a National Democratic Movement, recognizes the factions within its organization that wish to establish a progressive party. The factions formally announce their intention to do so on October 13, after seceding from the coalition.

27 The first preliminary meeting for both the 11th South-North Red Cross Talks and the second exchange of artists and home visitors is held at Panmunjom, marking the resumption of the inter-Korea dialogue after a six-month hiatus brought about by Reverend Moon Ik Hwan's visit to North Korea.

28 In a press conference in New York, the chief delegate of North Korea's UN observers proposes that in February 1990 both a "North-South summit" and a "political consultative meeting" be held by representatives of North and South Korean political parties and social organizations. Unlike North Korea's previous proposal, this one does not link the holding of a summit meeting to the abolition of South Korean anti-communist laws.

October

4 The Ministry of Defense announces that the 1989 joint military exercises between the USSR and North Korea took place in September. The exercises have been held annually since 1986.

6   A second preliminary meeting concerning the 11th South-North Red Cross talks and the second exchange of home visitors and artists is held at Panmunjom but ends without any significant agreement.

7   Pope John Paul II arrives in Seoul to attend the 44th World Eucharistic Congress, an international meeting of Roman Catholics held October 4–8.

9   U.S. Trade Representative Carla Hills arrives in Seoul for bilateral trade talks concerning such issues as Korea's importation of beef, the opening of the communications market, and the guarantee of intellectual property rights.

12   The third preliminary meeting concerning the establishment of South-North High-Level Talks is held at Panmunjom; no significant agreement is reached.

13   Six radical students attack the residence of the U.S. ambassador to Korea, demanding cancellation of President Roh's visit to the United States and condemning U.S. pressure that the Korean agricultural market be opened.

15   President Roh leaves Seoul for a five-day official visit to the United States.

16   In the third preliminary meeting at Panmunjom concerning the 11th South-North Red Cross talks and the second exchange of home visitors and artists, the two Koreas reach a basic understanding regarding the main talks, to be held on December 15 in Pyongyang, and the exchanges of visiting teams, to take place on December 9. (Subsequent meetings in November and December, however, fail to produce agreement upon specific procedures, the size of visiting groups, or the content of artistic performances.)

20   In the third South-North Sports Talks held at Panmunjom, "Korea" is adopted as the English name

of the joint team to be sent to the 1990 Asian Games in Beijing. The official song, flag, and English name of the joint team have now been agreed upon.

25   The eighth preliminary meeting concerning the South-North Parliamentary Conference is held at Panmunjom, the first in the ten months since December 29, 1988; no significant agreement is reached, however.

27   GATT resolves to exclude South Korea from the category of developing countries as defined in paragraph B of article XVIII of the GATT charter, which allows those countries to limit imports to help them manage their international balance of payments.

November

1   South Korea and Poland sign a protocol establishing a full diplomatic relationship.

3   A Japanese newspaper reports that Ho Dam will visit Washington in May 1990 to participate in a conference concerning the Korean peninsula.

5   North Korean President Kim Il Sung pays an unofficial three-day visit to Beijing. It is later reported that during this visit Kim, in meetings with Deng Xiaoping and Jiang Jimin, called for China's continued nonrecognition of South Korea and that Deng and Jiang agreed.

11   Police end a mass rally held in Seoul by six dissident organizations, including Chonminnyon, Chondaehyop, and Chonkyocho. The purpose of the rally is to demand the punishment of persons involved in the Kwangju incident and the so-called irregularities of the Fifth Republic, as well as to assert the right of the poor to subsistence and demand government recognition of Chonkyocho.

14   To boost declining business confidence and increase external competitiveness, the Roh government announces its first economic policy package, which provides for the lowering of interest rates, increasing of the money supply, adjustment of the exchange rate, and reestablishment of financial subsidiaries to exporters.

15   Two defecting North Korean students who had been studying in East Germany arrive in Seoul after passing through the newly opened Berlin Wall the previous week.

An estimated 10,000 police officers blockade a mass rally of farmers from around the country to demand an increase in the government procurement price for rice products.

16   In a press conference, the presidents of 6 major South Korean business associations, encompassing 30 business groups, announce the establishment of a united nationwide business organization to respond collectively to labor disputes. The association is established on December 23, in order to effectively coexist with Chonnoryon (the Coalition for a National Trade Union Movement), which was expected to be organized in early 1990.

17   South Korea and Czechoslovakia sign a protocol establishing trade offices in Seoul and Prague in 1990. Eastern European countries that have established trade offices in Seoul by this time are the Soviet Union, Hungary, Yugoslavia, Poland, and Bulgaria.

18   President Roh leaves Seoul to visit Hungary, West Germany, Great Britain, and France. He returns on December 4.

24   A Japanese newspaper reports that during his unofficial visit to Beijing North Korean President Kim Il Sung revealed to Deng Xiaoping his intention to resign and transfer his power to Kim Jong Il next year.

29   The ninth preliminary contact concerning the South-North Parliamentary Conference is held at Panmunjom but ends with agreement on only one point: that the matter of a nonaggression declaration is to be included on the agenda. The next meeting is scheduled for January 24, 1990.

December

6   The Soviet Union suggests that the Hyundai Business Group join the Siberian natural gas development project.

8   South Korea and the Soviet Union agree to establish consular departments in their trade offices in Seoul and Moscow in January 1990.

11   The South Korean government decides to establish a special committee to combat the current economic crisis.

14   The South Korean minister of sports announces that, beginning in 1990, South Korea and the Soviet Union will hold annual sports events, such as soccer, handball, and volleyball, alternately in their two countries.

15   In the Chong Wa Dae (presidential residence) meeting of President Roh Tae Woo, PPD President Kim Dae Jung, RDP President Kim Young Sam, and NDRP President Kim Jong Pil, the opposition leaders agree to bring to a conclusion two years of discussion of Fifth Republic irregularities and the Kwangju incident, mainly by requiring the testimony of former President Chun Doo Hwan before the combined Special National Assembly Committees and the resignation from office of Representative Chung Ho Yong.

18   Lim Jong Suk, chairman of Chondaehyop, is arrested.

19   The South Korean National Assembly ends its annual session. During the session, the fiscal 1990

budget was fixed at 22.6 trillion won (about US$33 billion), and the local autonomy law and laws concerning so-called public ownership of land were passed.

20   The South Korean national defense minister announces that his government has selected the FA18 rather than the F16 as its main fighter plane for the future. Twelve FA18s are to be imported from the United States in 1993, and by the late 1990s domestic industries are to assemble 36 FA18s and produce 72.

22   The last meeting in 1989 of the South-North Sports Talks concludes at Panmunjom, with agreement between the two Koreas on ten basic items to be discussed concerning the united Korean team to be sent to the 1990 Asian Games in Beijing. (The agreement eventually broke down, and in September 1990 two separate teams were sent to the games.)

To supplement its November 14 policy package, the government presents a proposal concerning the management of the South Korean economy in 1990, which includes the revival of a fund to support export industries, the depreciation of the Korean won, and an increase of subsidies to exporters. It is expected that total exports for 1989 will reach US$62 billion, far less than the original target of US$67 billion.

28   South Korea establishes diplomatic relations with Yugoslavia.

29   Representative Chung Ho Yong announces his intention to resign from his official positions.

31   Testifying before the National Assembly, former president Chun Doo Hwan denies responsibility for the Kwangju incident. Former president Choi Kyu Hah refuses to submit to the subpoena issued him on December 23.

Glossary

Common Abbreviations.
DJP: Democratic Justice Party
DLP: Democratic Liberal Party
DMZ: Demilitarized Zone
DP: Democratic Party
DPRK: Democratic People's Republic of Korea
NDRP: New Democratic-Republican Party
PPD: Party for Peace and Democracy
RDP: Reunification Democratic Party
ROK: Republic of Korea
WFYS: World Festival of Youth and Students

Armistice Agreement. An agreement to end the Korean War, signed at Panmunjom on July 27, 1953, by the UN Command (representing UN, U.S., and South Korean forces), on the one side, and the Supreme Commander of the Korean People's Army and the Commander of the Chinese People's Volunteers, on the other. The purpose of the agreement was to "insure a complete cessation of hostile and of all acts of armed forces in Korea until a peaceful settlement is achieved." No permanent peace treaty replacing this supposedly temporary truce has yet been negotiated.

"Asian Tigers." Term used to describe the four major newly industrialized countries (NICs) in the Pacific region: Hong Kong, Singapore, South Korea, and Taiwan.

Choi Kyu Hah. Caretaker president of the Republic of Korea from the time of *Park Chung Hee*'s assassination in October 1979 until Choi's controversial resignation in favor of *Chun Doo Hwan* in 1980. During Choi's term, the *December 12 coup of 1979* and the *Kwangju incident* took place. Subpoenaed to testify before the National Assembly in December, he failed to appear. Choi has never publicly explained his role in these events.

Chun Doo Hwan. President of the *Fifth Republic* of Korea, 1980–88. Chun was commander of the Defense Security Command, an army intelligence unit in Seoul, at the time of President *Park Chung Hee's* assassination on October 26, 1979. Chun initiated the *December 12 coup of 1979*, with the assistance of General *Roh Tae Woo* and other Korea Military Academy classmates, mainly against Army Chief of Staff Chung Sung Hwa. After the unexplained resignation of then president *Choi Kyu Hah*, Chun was chosen by the electoral college in August 1980 and re-elected to a seven-year term in February 1981 by a newly formed electoral college under a revised constitution. He stepped down in February 1988, in the first change of power through presidential election in the nation's 40-year history. During Chun's term, the so-called *Fifth Republic* irregularities—for example, Chun's relatives' illegal economic activities—overshadowed his achievement in leading the nation to economic recovery. On December 31, 1989, Chun testified before the National Assembly on the Fifth Republic irregularities and the *Kwangju incident*.

Chung Ho Yong. National Assemblyman of the ruling *Democratic Justice Party*, he was commander of Airborne Special Forces Command during the *Kwangju incident* of May 1980 and a Korea Military Academy classmate of former president *Chun Doo Hwan* and President *Roh Tae Woo*. Chung was forced to resign from the National Assembly after his December 1989 testimony before the Special House Committees, in which he accepted responsibility for the Kwangju incident but neither admitted wrongdoing nor showed remorse.

Chung Ju Yung. Founder and honorary chairman of the Hyundai Business Group, he has played a significant role in the *Roh Tae Woo* government's *Nordpolitik,* especially in the effort to establish relationships with the USSR.

December 12 Coup of 1979. Coup initiated by Commander of the Defense Security Command *Chun Doo Hwan*, with the assistance of Korea Military Academy classmates such as General *Roh Tae Woo*, against the Army Chief of Staff and Commander of Martial Law Command Chung Sung Hwa. Apparently it was a struggle between two competing generational factions in the army rather than what the coup leaders later described as a "patriotic act to save the nation."

Demilitarized Zone (DMZ). An area of two kilometers on both sides of the Military Demarcation Line, 155 miles long, that is the border between South and North Korea. The DMZ was set aside by the *Armistice Agreement* of July 27, 1953, as a buffer zone to prevent an outbreak of hostilities.

Democratic Justice Party (DJP). Established in 1981 by President *Chun Doo Hwan*. *Roh Tae Woo* became its chairman in 1985. On January 22, 1990, President Roh announced the merger of the DJP with two of the three opposition parties, the *NDRP* and the *RDP*. At the time of the merger, the DJP held 127 seats in the 299-member National Assembly.

Democratic Liberal Party (DLP). Formed by the merger of the *DJP*, *NDRP*, and *RDP*, it commands a more than two-thirds majority in the National Assembly.

Democratic Party (DP). Established in early 1990 as an opposition party, after two of the three former opposition parties had merged with the ruling *DJP* to form the *DLP*. Its leader is *Lee Ki Taek*.

Democratic People's Republic of Korea (DPRK). Official name of North Korea.

Elections. The 13th Presidential Election of December 16, 1987, was the first direct election for president since 1971. *DJP* candidate *Roh Tae Woo* secured 36.6 percent of the vote, trailed by *Kim Young Sam* of the *RPD* (28 percent), *Kim Dae Jung* of the *PPD* (27 percent), and *Kim Jong Pil* of the *NDRP* (8.1 percent).

   The 13th National Assembly Election of April 27, 1988, resulted in 125 seats for the *DJP*, 71 seats for the *PPD*, 59 seats for the *RPD*, 35 seats for the *NDRP*, and 9 seats for other parties.

Fifth Republic. The *Chun Doo Hwan* regime, 1980–88.

Ho Dam. Former minister of foreign affairs of North Korea, he is currently chairman of the Committee for Peaceful Reunification of the Fatherland, a North Korean organization that conducts dialogue with the South, and secretary of the Korean Workers' Party.

July 1988 Declaration. Announcement by President *Roh Tae Woo* of a package of policies designed to put an end to the antagonism between Seoul and Pyongyang and expedite reunification of the Korean peninsula.

June 1987 Declaration. Surprise announcement by *Roh Tae Woo*, then a presidential candidate handpicked by President *Chun Doo Hwan*, of an "eight-point democratization package" that accepted every

demand of the opposition, including constitutional revision leading to direct presidential elections. Chun endorsed Roh's democratization formula on July 1, 1987.

Kim Dae Jung. Leader of the opposition *PPD*. Kim was convicted on
sedition charges in 1980 just before the start of *Chun Doo Hwan's*
Fifth Republic government, which gave him a suspended 20-year
prison sentence, stripped him of his civil rights, and banned him
from politics. Then DJP chairman *Roh Tae Woo's June 1987 Declaration* restored Kim's civil rights and enabled him to establish his
party in time for the presidential *election* of December 1987, in
which he won 27 percent of the vote.

Kim Il Sung. Leader of the *Democratic People's Republic of Korea* since
1945.

Kim Jong Il. The son of *Kim Il Sung*, being groomed as successor to
his father. He was appointed first vice chairman of the National
Defense Commission, his highest government post to date, in
May 1990. Kim Jong Il's successful replacement of his father
would be the first dynastic succession to occur in a communist
country.

Kim Jong Pil. Vice president of the *Democratic Liberal Party*. Leader of
the *New Democratic-Republican Party* at the time of its merger with
the ruling *DJP* and the *RDP*, Kim played a role in planning the
1961 coup by General *Park Chung Hee* and set up the Democratic
Republican Party, which governed from 1961 to 1979. He also established the Korean Central Intelligence Agency (KCIA) in 1961.
In the National Assembly *elections* of April 1988, the NDRP won
only 35 seats of the total 299.

Kim Young Sam. Executive chairman of the *Democratic Liberal Party*.
Leader of the *Reunification Democratic Party* at the time of its
merger with the *DJP* and the *NDRP*, Kim was president of the
opposition New Democratic Party during the *Park Chung Hee* regime and also led the opposition to *Chun Doo Hwan*. In the presidential election of December 1987, Kim won 28 percent of the
vote.

Kwangju Incident. A violent 10-day confrontation in May 1980 between *ROK* special forces troops and anti-martial law demonstrators in Kwangju, South Cholla province. The May 1980 blood-
bath, in which at least 192 people died, opened wounds in
volatile Cholla province that still fester today. The roots of the
uprising lay in the assassination of President *Park Chung Hee* on

October 26, 1979, the political vacuum left by his death, and the subsequent *December 12 coup* by Commander of the Defense Security Command *Chun Doo Hwan* along with General *Roh Tae Woo* and other Korea Military Academy graduates and their followers. The question of who ordered the troops to fire on the demonstrators has not yet been answered.

Lee Ki Taek. Leader of the newly established *Democratic Party*.

National Security Law. Enacted in 1958 to control the activities of "anti-state" organizations. The law's ostensible purpose is to protect national security, but it has frequently been applied selectively to punish domestic dissidents. Among its most controversial provisions is one forbidding travel by South Korean citizens to North Korea.

New Democratic-Republican Party (NDRP). The minority opposition party of *Kim Jong Pil* until it merged with the *DJP* and the *RDP* in January 1990 to form a new majority party, the *DLP*.

Nordpolitik, **or Northern Policy.** A term to describe the *Roh Tae Woo* government's diplomatic strategy since the *July 1988 Declaration* to establish economic and diplomatic relationships with other communist bloc countries. South Korea has recently established full diplomatic relationships with Hungary, Poland, Yugoslavia, Romania, Mongolia, and (as of September 30, 1990) the USSR.

Park Chung Hee. President of Korea from 1961 to 1979. In 1972 Park instituted the Yushin Constitution, under which he became the first indirectly elected president of the *ROK*, chosen by an electoral college called the National Conference for Unification for a six-year term of office. Park was assassinated by KCIA director Kim Chae Kyu on October 26, 1979.

Party for Peace and Democracy (PPD). The only remaining major opposition party in the National Assembly, with 70 seats of the total 299. *Kim Dae Jung* is its president.

Republic of Korea (ROK). Official name of South Korea.

Reunification Democratic Party (RDP). The second-largest opposition party until it merged with the *DJP* and the *NDRP* in January 1990 to form the majority *DLP*. *Kim Young Sam* was its president.

Roh Tae Woo. Since 1988, president of the *Republic of Korea*. During the *Fifth Republic*, Roh was minister of home affairs, minister of sports, chairman of the Seoul Olympics Organizing Committee and, from 1985–1990, chairman of the *Democratic Justice Party*. Currently leader of the newly established *Democratic Liberal Party*.

Status of U.S. Armed Forces in Korea Agreement. The agreement covering U.S. military facilities and jurisdiction over U.S. military personnel suspected of crimes committed in Korea, signed in 1966. There is a growing outcry in South Korea for amending the agreement.

Syngman Rhee. The *ROK's* first president (1948–60), whose Liberal Party administration was toppled by a student uprising in April 1960.

"Team Spirit." Annual joint military exercise between South Korea and the United States since 1976. In recent years, it has usually involved about 140,000 South Korean soldiers and 60,000 Americans; however, with the current U.S. defense budget cuts on overseas exercises, the scale of the "Spirit" is expected to decrease.

World Festival of Youth and Students (WFYS). Launched in Prague, Czechoslovkia, in July 1947, with the slogan, "Youth, unite in the struggle for a durable and lasting peace," the 13th WFYS was held in Pyongyang, North Korea, from July 1 through July 9, 1989. In 1973 the current slogan, "For anti-imperialist solidarity, peace, and friendship," was adopted.

Suggestions for Further Reading

A Strategic Framework for the Asian Pacific Rim: Looking Toward the 21st Century, Report of the Defense Department to the Congress, April 1990.

Cho, Myung Hyun, "The New Student Movement in Korea: Emerging Patterns of Ideological Orientation in the 1980's," *Korea Observer*, Vol. 20, no. 1 (September 1989), pp. 93–125.

Clark, Donald N., ed., *The Kwangju Uprising* (Boulder, CO: Westview Press, 1988).

Clough, Ralph N., *Embattled Korea* (Boulder, CO: Westview Press, 1987).

Collins, Susan M., and Won-Am Park, "External Debt and Macroeconomic Performance in South Korea," in Jeffrey D. Sachs and Susan M. Collins, eds., *Developing Country Debt and Economic Performance*, Vol. 3 (Chicago: University of Chicago Press, 1989), pp. 153–369.

Han, Sung-Joo, "South Korea in 1987—The Politics of Democratization," *Asian Survey* (January 1988).

Han, Sung-Joo, "South Korea in 1988—A Revolution in the Making," *Asian Survey* (January 1989).

Han, Sung-Joo, "South Korea: Politics in Transition," in Larry Diamond, Juan J. Linz, and Seymour Martin Lipset, eds., *Democracy in Developing Countries: Asia* (Boulder, CO: Lynne Rienner Publishers, 1989).

Industrial East Asia: Tasks and Challenges (Seoul: The Korean Sociological Association, 1989).

Kihl, Young Whan, "South Korea in 1989: Slow Progress Toward Democracy," *Asian Survey* (January 1990).

Kim, Hak-Joon, *The Unification Policy of South and North Korea: A Comparative Study* (Seoul: Seoul National University Press, 1977).

161

Kim, Ilpyong, and Y. W. Kihl, eds., *Political Change in South Korea* (New York: Pagan House, 1988).

Koh, Byung Chul, *The Foreign Policy Systems of North and South Korea* (Berkeley: University of California Press, 1984).

Koh, Byung Chul, *A Midterm Assessment of the Roh Tae Woo Government* (New York: The Asia Society, 1990).

Korea at the Crossroads: Implications for American Policy (New York: The Asia Society and Council on Foreign Relations, 1987).

Korea's Macroeconomic and Financial Policies, papers presented at the joint KDI/IIE Conference on Korean Financial Policy (Seoul: Korea Development Institute, 1989).

Kwon, Tai Hwan, "Perceptions of the Quality of Life and Social Conflicts," *Korea Journal,* Vol. 29, no. 9 (September 1989), pp. 5–31.

Lee, Chong-Sik, *Korean Workers' Party: A Short History* (Stanford, CA: Hoover Institution Press, 1978).

Macdonald, Donald Stone, *The Koreans: Contemporary Politics and Society,* second ed. (Boulder, CO: Westview Press, 1990).

Rauenhorst, Amu M., *Industrial Relations in the Republic of Korea,* M.A. thesis, The Fletcher School of Law and Diplomacy, Medford, MA, 1989.

Scalapino, Robert A., and Chong-Sik Lee, *Communism in Korea* (Berkeley: University of California Press, 1973), 2 vols.

Sohn, Hak-kyu, "Development of the Human Rights Movement Under the Yushin Regime," *Korea Social Science Journal,* Vol. 15 (1989), pp. 41–63.

Suh, Dae-Sook, *Kim Il Sung: The North Korean Leader* (New York: Columbia University Press, 1988).

Yang, Sung Chul, *Korea and Two Regimes* (Cambridge, MA: Schenkman Publishing Co., 1981).

Young, Soogil, "New Challenges to the Korean Economy and their International Implications," KDI Working Paper (April 1990).

About the Contributors

Byung-Joon Ahn is Professor of Political Science at Yonsei University, Seoul. He is the author of *Chinese Politics and the Cultural Revolution* (1976) and coeditor with Jae Kyu Park of *The Strategic Defense Initiative: Its Implications for Asia and the Pacific* (1987).

Vincent S. R. Brandt is a freelance social anthropologist who does occasional teaching, consulting, and research on Korea. His publications include *A Korean Village: Between Farm and Sea*, published by Harvard University Press (1971) and *Planning from the Bottom Up: Community-Based Integrated Rural Development in South Korea*, with Ji Woong Cheong (1979). He is currently interested in contemporary social change in Northeast Asia.

Sung-Joo Han is Professor of Political Science at Korea University, Seoul. He graduated from Seoul National University in 1962 and received a Ph.D. degree from the University of California, Berkeley, in 1970. After teaching in the United States, he joined the faculty of Korea University where he also served as director of the Asiatic Research Center. He is the author of *The Failure of Democracy in South Korea* (1974) and coauthor of *Foreign Policy of the Republic of Korea* (1985).

Michael C. Kalton is Professor of East Asian Philosophy and Religion at the Universtiy of Washington at Tacoma. His research specialization is Korean Confucianism, and in 1987 he was awarded the International T'oegye Studies Prize for his book *To Become a Sage: The Ten Diagrams on Sage Learning by Yi T'oegye*, published by Columbia University Press (1988). As a corollary to his research and publications dealing with traditional Confucianism he has increasingly become engaged in consideration of the impact of the Confucian heritage on modernization and economic development in contemporary East Asia and its promise for the next century.

Seong-Kon Kim is Associate Professor of English at Seoul National University. He was educated at Columbia University and the State University of New York at Buffalo, where he received his Ph.D. degree. Editor of a prestigious literary quarterly in Korean, *Contemporary World Literature*, his recent books include *Journey into the Past* (1985), *Words in the Labyrinth* (1986), *Simple Etiquette in Korea* (1988), *American Literature in the Postmodern Age* (1989), and *Postmodernism and Contemporary American Literature* (1990). Awarded a Fulbright Senior Research Grant and a Fulbright Scholar-in-Residence Grant, he currently teaches at Pennsylvania State University as a Visiting Professor.

Bon-Ho Koo is currently the president of the Korea Development Institute in Seoul, which is an autonomous, policy-oriented research organization established by the Korean government. He has contributed chapters to *Korea-U.S. Relations: The Politics of Trade and Security* (1988), *Korean Economic Development* (1990), and *Economic Cooperation in the Asia-Pacific Region* (1990).

Chong-Sik Lee is Professor of Political Science at the University of Pennsylvania. His publications include *The Politics of Korean Nationalism* (1963), *Communism in Korea*, coauthored with Robert A. Scalapino (1973), *Korean Workers' Party: A Short History* (1978), *Revolutionary Struggle in Manchuria: Chinese Communism and Soviet Interest, 1922–1945* (1983), and *Japan and Korea: The Political Dimension* (1985).

Index